Canadian Living
Fish & Seafood

EXCLUSIVE DISTRIBUTOR FOR CANADA & USA
Simon & Schuster Canada
166 King Street East, Suite 300
Toronto ON M5A 1J3
Tel: 647-427-8882
Toll Free: 800-387-0446   **simonandschuster.ca**
Fax: 647-430-9446   **canadianliving.com/books**

Cataloguing data available from
Bibliothèque et Archives nationales du Québec.

Art director: Colin Elliott
Project editor: Tina Anson Mine
Copy editor: Lisa Fielding
Indexer: Beth Zabloski

04-16

Legal deposit: 2016
Bibliothèque et Archives nationales du Québec
Library and Archives Canada

ISBN 978-1-988002-28-6

Printed in Canada

Government of Quebec – Tax credit for book publishing –
Administered by SODEC.
sodec.gouv.qc.ca

This publisher gratefully acknowledges the support of the
Société de développement des enterprises culturelles du Québec.

 Canada Council   Conseil des arts
for the Arts   du Canada

We gratefully acknowledge the support of the
Canada Council for the Arts for its publishing program.

Financé par le gouvernement du Canada   **Canadä**
Funded by the Government of Canada

We acknowledge the financial support of our publishing activities
by the Government of Canada through the Canada Book Fund.

Canadian Living
Fish & Seafood

BY THE CANADIAN LIVING TEST KITCHEN

JUNIPER
PUBLISHING
A Quebecor Media Corporation

From Our Test Kitchen

In Canada, we are lucky enough to have access to some of the freshest, most high-quality ingredients in the world—and our fish and seafood may be the best example. From cold Maritime waters come the mellowest mussels and clams, the sweetest oysters and the tastiest lobsters. From the west coast comes a huge assortment of saltwater delights, including rich sockeye salmon, buttery sablefish and sweet, briny spot prawns. The Arctic Ocean provides even more unique varieties, such as rich, velvety arctic char. The lakes and rivers that run inside the boundaries of these three coasts are home to dozens of types of freshwater fish, such as meaty, mild pickerel and tender, flavourful trout.

In this book, you'll find 110 of our tastiest Tested-Till-Perfect recipes that feature these local, iconic fish and seafood varieties, as well as other offerings from around the globe. We've also helped you search out the most sustainable options, so you can be confident you're choosing ingredients that protect not just our waters but also oceans, rivers and lakes worldwide. This will help you ensure these bodies of water stay a rich source of food for decades to come.

Eat well and enjoy!

Annabelle

ANNABELLE WAUGH
FOOD DIRECTOR

Spicy Asian
Crab Noodle Salad
page 68

Our Tested-Till-Perfect guarantee means we've
tested every recipe, using the same grocery store
ingredients and household appliances as you do,
until we're sure you'll get perfect results at home.

CANADIAN LIVING
TESTED
TILL
PERFECT
EST. 1975
TEST KITCHEN

Canada's Food Guide recommends that Canadians consume at least two 75 g portions of fish or seafood per week.

Contents

# Fish & Seafood Basics

BUYING & STORING

The Canadian Living Test Kitchen cooks a lot of fish and seafood every year. Here are a few of our top tips for purchasing and storing these tasty ingredients.

Know the Seller » Buy fish and seafood from a fish counter or market with high turnover; ask what is freshest, and adjust your menu accordingly. Buy seafood from a shop you trust, and try to develop a relationship with the fishmonger.

Take a Sniff » Fish should have a neutral aroma. If it smells fishy, it's not fresh.

Look Closely » Whole fish should be firm, with bright red gills, clear eyes and scales that adhere tightly. Fish fillets and steaks should be moist and elastic throughout, with no dry or discoloured edges.

Broaden Your Palate » Try to enjoy all types of fish, not just top-feeding predators such as tuna, salmon and halibut. Try mussels, clams, oysters, cod, mackerel, and trout...the options are endless.

Use It Quickly » Whenever possible, cook fish the same day you buy it. Wrap it in plastic wrap and keep it in the coldest part of the refrigerator, preferably on ice. You can store fish for a day or two; simply wrap it in paper towels and change them after 24 hours.

Great sustainable choices!
CLAMS, BAY SCALLOPS & FARMED MUSSELS

SWITCH TO SUSTAINABLE

Buying sustainable seafood is smart: It helps ensure fish stocks will be there for future generations. Many popular varieties that are readily available are unsustainably farmed or harvested—check the chart below for some eco-friendly alternatives. Keep in mind that the ratings for different kinds of seafood change over time; for up-to-date information on sustainable options, visit **oceanwise.ca.**

WHAT ABOUT FARMED?

Farmed fish are often raised using environmentally destructive methods (Atlantic salmon is one of the worst culprits), including antibiotics, artificial colourants and genetically modified feed. But sustainable fisheries do exist. Off-bottom mollusk farming (mussels, clams, scallops and oysters) generally involves no feed; only the seeding and harvesting happen in areas near shore. Mollusks are also filters that contribute positively to the ocean environment, so they are beneficial.

Facts on Origins & Fishing Methods

Some common fishing practices threaten marine life, and some species are overfished. A little knowledge about their origins will help you enjoy fish and shellfish with less worry about environmental impact.

Salmon	Mackerel	Arctic char	Tilapia	Crab	Tuna	Shrimp	Sardines
↓ CHOOSE ↓	↓ CHOOSE ↓	↓ CHOOSE ↓	↓ CHOOSE ↓	↓ CHOOSE ↓	↓ CHOOSE ↓	↓ CHOOSE ↓	↓ CHOOSE ↓
Wild Alaskan or land/closed-containment farmed	Wild Atlantic mackerel from the U.S. and Canada, or king or Spanish mackerel from the U.S.	Closed-system farmed	Closed-system farmed from the U.S. or Canada, or raceway farmed from Peru	Wild snow crab from Alaska or the Gulf of St. Lawrence, or Dungeness crab from Alaska or B.C.	Pole- or troll-caught wild albacore from Canada or the Pacific U.S.	Spot prawns from B.C., or prawns or shrimp certified by the Aquaculture Stewardship Council (ASC)	Wild Pacific from Canada or the Pacific U.S.

Source: Oceanwise.ca

HINT » Less is more: a 140 g serving
of fish per person is plenty.

MAKE IT EASY

Whole fish are messy and time-consuming to prep
for cooking. Ask your fishmonger to scale and clean
the fish, and remove the gills. Then it will be ready
to use as soon as you get home.

TECHNIQUE: SERVING WHOLE FISH

Whether grilled, broiled, baked or steamed, a whole
fish is juicy and flavourful. Plus, it's a real showstopper
when you place it on the table in front of guests. Here's
how we serve a cooked whole fish without any flaky bits.

1   Using a thin, sharp filleting knife, run
the blade along the spine of the fish and
around the head (if still attached) to release
the top fillet (the side of the fish facing you).

2   If the fish is large enough to serve more
than one person, cut the top fillet crosswise
into portion-size pieces.

3   Use a thin, firm but flexible spatula (or a
slotted spatula-like tool called a fish slice).
Starting at the thicker (head) end of the fish,
slide it between the top fillet and the bones.
Gently lift the fillet off and serve.

4   Flip the fish over and repeat steps 1 to 3.
Alternatively, don't flip it over and, using
your fingers, gently lift the spine and bones
off the bottom fillet and discard. Cut the
fillet into portion-size pieces and serve.

HINT » When you're serving
lobster, put a pair or two
of sharp kitchen shears
on the table along with
the lobster crackers and
picks. They're great for
cutting open the claws
and tail so you can get
at that sweet meat.

GRILLING: TEXTURE IS KEY

The best whole fish for grilling have firm or flaky
(but not soft) flesh and skin that will crisp nicely;
go for pickerel, whitefish, salmon, trout, arctic char,
bass or snapper. Fillets and steaks from almost
any fish will work, except soft-fleshed species,
such as cod, flounder, sole or fluke. Cook these
delicate options in foil packets on the barbecue .

HINT » If you're buying oysters
from the grocery store,
check the harvest date on
the box: one to two weeks
out of water is fine.

Shrimp and Green Onion Mini-Pancakes

HANDS-ON TIME	•	TOTAL TIME	•	MAKES
45 MINUTES		45 MINUTES		ABOUT 48 PIECES

What you need

GARLIC SOY SAUCE:

¼ cup	soy sauce
4 tsp	unseasoned rice vinegar
2 tsp	sesame oil
2	cloves garlic, minced

PANCAKES:

2 cups	all-purpose flour
2 tbsp	cornstarch
½ tsp	salt
2 cups	ice water
2	eggs, lightly beaten
2 cups	shrimp, peeled, deveined and chopped (see tip, below)
4	green onions, chopped
2	red finger chili peppers or jalapeño peppers, seeded and thinly sliced
3 tbsp	vegetable oil

How to make it

GARLIC SOY SAUCE: Stir together soy sauce, vinegar, sesame oil and garlic; set aside.

PANCAKES: In large bowl, whisk together flour, cornstarch and salt; stir in ice water until smooth. Whisk in eggs just until blended. Stir in shrimp, green onions and chili peppers.

In cast-iron or nonstick skillet, heat 1 tbsp of the oil over medium heat; using 1 tbsp per pancake, spoon batter into pan. Cook, turning once, until top is set and bottom is golden, about 6 minutes. Repeat with remaining oil and batter.

Serve Pancakes hot or at room temperature with Garlic Soy Sauce.

TIP FROM THE TEST KITCHEN
Any size shrimp will work in this recipe, because they need to be chopped. Go ahead and buy more economical small shrimp.

NUTRITIONAL INFORMATION, PER PIECE: about 39 cal, 2 g pro, 1 g total fat (trace sat. fat), 5 g carb, trace fibre, 15 mg chol, 109 mg sodium, 25 mg potassium. % RDI: 1% calcium, 3% iron, 1% vit A, 2% vit C, 6% folate.

Shrimp Spring Rolls

HANDS-ON TIME		TOTAL TIME		MAKES
35 MINUTES	•	35 MINUTES	•	16 PIECES

What you need

DIPPING SAUCE:

3 tbsp	unseasoned rice vinegar
1 tbsp	matchstick-cut fresh ginger
2 tsp	granulated sugar
½ tsp	minced seeded red finger chili pepper
pinch	salt

SPRING ROLLS:

450 g	shrimp (see tip, page 11), peeled and deveined
1	can (227 mL) water chestnuts, drained and chopped
1	green onion, minced
¼ cup	chopped fresh cilantro
½ tsp	finely grated fresh ginger
½ tsp	salt
pinch	white pepper
16	square (6-inch/15 cm) spring roll wrappers
1	egg, lightly beaten
	vegetable oil for frying

How to make it

DIPPING SAUCE: Stir together vinegar, ginger, sugar, chili pepper, salt and 2 tbsp water until sugar is dissolved. Set aside.

SPRING ROLLS: On cutting board, cover shrimp with plastic wrap; using bottom of saucepan, pound until flattened and broken up. Transfer shrimp to bowl. Stir in water chestnuts, green onion, cilantro, ginger, salt and pepper until well combined.

Lay 1 spring roll wrapper on work surface with point up; shape 2 tbsp of the shrimp mixture into 3-inch (8 cm) long log across bottom third of wrapper. Roll up, folding in sides, until only 1-inch (2.5 cm) triangle of wrapper remains. Lightly brush triangle with egg; roll up to seal. Repeat with remaining shrimp mixture, wrappers and egg. *(Make-ahead: Refrigerate on parchment paper–lined rimmed baking sheet for up to 2 hours.)*

Pour enough oil into heavy-bottomed skillet to come ½ inch (1 cm) up side; heat over medium-high heat just until ripples appear on surface. Reduce heat to medium; working in batches, fry spring rolls, turning often and increasing heat if necessary, until golden and filling is pink and opaque in centre, 3 to 4 minutes per batch. Using slotted spoon, transfer to paper towel–lined plate; let drain. Serve with Dipping Sauce.

TIP FROM THE TEST KITCHEN

Tiny bits of the wrappers may break off when you're frying the rolls. This won't affect the rolls, but those small pieces can burn if they remain in the skillet. Simply skim the oil between batches to remove them.

NUTRITIONAL INFORMATION, PER PIECE: about 112 cal, 6 g pro, 5 g total fat (1 g sat. fat), 10 g carb, trace fibre, 44 mg chol, 167 mg sodium, 60 mg potassium. % RDI: 1% calcium, 4% iron, 2% vit A, 2% vit C, 2% folate.

Spanish Salt Cod Fritters

HANDS-ON TIME	•	TOTAL TIME	•	MAKES
50 MINUTES		37¼ HOURS		ABOUT 46 PIECES

What you need

400 g	bone-in salt cod, cut in 4 pieces
675 g	russet potatoes, peeled and quartered
3 tbsp	extra-virgin olive oil
¼ cup	all-purpose flour
3	eggs
⅓ cup	finely chopped green onions
⅓ cup	chopped fresh parsley
1	clove garlic, minced
¼ tsp	pepper
	vegetable oil for frying

How to make it

Rinse fish well under cold water. Place in large deep bowl; cover with cold water. Cover and refrigerate for 36 hours, changing water 4 times. Taste fish; if still too salty, continue changing water and soaking for up to 8 hours longer. Drain and rinse fish.

In saucepan, combine fish and enough cold water to cover; bring to simmer over medium-high heat. Turn off heat; let stand until fish flakes easily when tested, about 20 minutes. Reserving cooking liquid, drain fish well; let cool. Discard skin and bones; flake fish. Set aside.

In saucepan, combine reserved cooking liquid and potatoes; bring to boil. Cook potatoes until tender, about 15 minutes. Drain; return to pan over medium-low heat to dry for 30 seconds. Mash potatoes; transfer to bowl.

In clean saucepan, bring olive oil and ¾ cup water to boil over medium heat; vigorously whisk in flour until smooth, about 2 minutes. Remove from heat. Whisk for 1 minute. Whisk in eggs, 1 at a time. Stir in potatoes. Add green onions, parsley, garlic and pepper; stir in fish just until combined. Let cool.

Pour enough vegetable oil into Dutch oven to come 2 inches (5 cm) up side; heat until deep-fryer thermometer reads 375°F (190°C). Drop fish mixture by heaping 1 tbsp into hot oil; deep-fry, turning once, until golden brown, 4 to 5 minutes. Transfer to rack set over baking sheet; let drain.

NUTRITIONAL INFORMATION, PER PIECE: about 114 cal, 6 g pro, 9 g total fat (1 g sat. fat), 3 g carb, trace fibre, 25 mg chol, 583 mg sodium, 159 mg potassium. % RDI: 2% calcium, 3% iron, 1% vit A, 3% vit C, 3% folate.

Avocado and Shrimp Cocktail

HANDS-ON TIME	•	TOTAL TIME	•	MAKES
20 MINUTES		20 MINUTES		4 SERVINGS

What you need

half	lemon
half	onion
450 g	large shrimp (31 to 40 count), peeled and deveined (see tip, below)
¼ cup	lime juice
2 tbsp	olive oil
¼ tsp	salt
¼ tsp	cayenne-based hot pepper sauce (such as Tabasco)
1	avocado, pitted, peeled and diced
1 cup	cherry tomatoes, halved
¼ cup	chopped fresh cilantro
3 tbsp	finely chopped red onion

How to make it

Juice lemon. In large saucepan of cold water, combine lemon juice, squeezed lemon and onion. Bring to boil. Add shrimp; cook until pink and opaque throughout, about 2 minutes. Drain shrimp, discarding lemon and onion; rinse under cold water and drain again. Cut shrimp in half crosswise.

In large bowl, stir together lime juice, oil, salt and hot pepper sauce. Gently stir in shrimp, avocado, cherry tomatoes, cilantro and red onion.

Spoon into cocktail glasses.

TIP FROM THE TEST KITCHEN
The names of shrimp sizes, such as "large" or "jumbo," aren't standardized. That's why we also provide the count in our ingredient lists. This tells you how many pieces you'll get in a 450 g portion.

NUTRITIONAL INFORMATION, PER SERVING: about 242 cal, 19 g pro, 16 g total fat (2 g sat. fat), 8 g carb, 4 g fibre, 128 mg chol, 279 mg sodium, 514 mg potassium. % RDI: 5% calcium, 18% iron, 8% vit A, 22% vit C, 26% folate.

Avocado is very delicate,
so stir it in gently to keep
the cubes intact.

Invest in a sturdy, high-quality oyster knife. It won't slip as much and will help keep your fingers safe when shucking.

Oysters on the Half Shell

HANDS-ON TIME	TOTAL TIME	MAKES
15 MINUTES	15 MINUTES	8 SERVINGS

What you need

16	oysters
	hot pepper sauce
	lemon wedges
	grated fresh horseradish (optional)

How to make it

Using stiff brush, scrub oysters under cold running water. Using thick cloth or glove, hold oyster, curved part of shell down; insert oyster knife into small opening near hinge. Twist knife to break hinge; wipe blade clean.

Reinsert knife and slide along underside of top shell to cut through muscle; discard top shell, removing any grit or broken shell on oyster.

Keeping oyster level to retain juices, slide knife under oyster to cut through bottom muscle. Repeat with remaining oysters, wiping knife clean between each.

Serve in shells with hot pepper sauce, lemon wedges, and horseradish (if using).

NUTRITIONAL INFORMATION, PER SERVING: about 19 cal, 2 g pro, 1 g total fat (trace sat. fat), 1 g carb, 0 g fibre, 15 mg chol, 59 mg sodium, 44 mg potassium. % RDI: 1% calcium, 14% iron, 1% vit A, 2% vit C, 1% folate.

Tuna Tartare

HANDS-ON TIME	TOTAL TIME	MAKES
10 MINUTES	10 MINUTES	24 SERVINGS

What you need

340 g	sushi-grade fresh tuna, diced
¼ cup	finely diced red onion
2 tbsp	minced fresh parsley
1 tbsp	minced drained capers
2 tsp	each Worcestershire sauce and Dijon mustard
1 tsp	lemon juice
pinch	each salt and pepper
	croûtes or baguette slices (optional)

How to make it

In bowl, stir together tuna, red onion, parsley, capers, Worcestershire sauce, mustard, lemon juice, salt and pepper. Serve immediately, on croûtes (if using).

NUTRITIONAL INFORMATION, PER SERVING: about 22 cal, 3 g pro, 1 g total fat (trace sat. fat), trace carb, trace fibre, 5 mg chol, 37 mg sodium, 44 mg potassium. % RDI: 1% iron, 10% vit A, 2% vit C.

Maple-Mustard Smoked Trout

HANDS-ON TIME	•	**TOTAL TIME**	•	**MAKES**
15 MINUTES		3¼ HOURS		8 TO 10 SERVINGS

What you need

¼ cup	grainy mustard
2 tbsp	maple syrup
1 tsp	grated lemon zest
1 tbsp	lemon juice
1 tsp	chopped fresh thyme
2	cloves garlic, finely chopped
½ tsp	coarse salt
½ tsp	freshly ground black pepper
900 g	skin-on rainbow trout or artic char fillets (about 3)

How to make it

Soak 2 cups wood chips (see tip, below) in water for 1 hour; drain. Seal wood chips in foil to make packet; poke several holes in top of packet.

Set foil drip pan under 1 rack of 2-burner barbecue or under centre rack of 3-burner barbecue. Heat remaining burner(s) to medium-low. Place packet of wood chips over lit burner. (For charcoal grill, set drip pan under 1 side of grill and arrange hot coals on other side. Place packet directly on coals.) Close lid and let smoke fill barbecue.

Meanwhile, in small bowl, whisk together mustard, maple syrup, lemon zest, lemon juice, thyme, garlic, salt and pepper; set aside.

Place fish, skin side down, on greased grill over drip pan; brush with half of the mustard mixture. Close lid and grill until fish flakes easily when tested, about 2 hours, basting with remaining mustard mixture during last 30 minutes of cooking.

TIP FROM THE TEST KITCHEN
Each type of wood has its own unique flavour. Hickory and mesquite are potent; maple, apple, cherry and alder are milder. Look for food-grade wood chips at hardware stores and garden centres.

NUTRITIONAL INFORMATION, PER EACH OF 10 SERVINGS:
about 129 cal, 17 g pro, 5 g total fat (1 g sat. fat), 3 g carb, trace fibre, 48 mg chol, 187 mg sodium, 388 mg potassium. % RDI: 6% calcium, 3% iron, 6% vit A, 5% vit C, 4% folate.

If the trout skin gets stuck to your grill, slide the fish off the skin and directly onto your serving platter.

Rice Paper Lobster Rolls

HANDS-ON TIME	TOTAL TIME	MAKES
50 MINUTES	50 MINUTES	24 PIECES

What you need

DIPPING SAUCE:

¼ cup	sweet Thai chili sauce
2 tbsp	unseasoned rice vinegar
1 tsp	fish sauce

RICE PAPER ROLLS:

1	live lobster (about 450 g), see tip, below
12	large leaves fresh mint, sliced
½ cup	thinly sliced sweet red pepper
½ cup	thinly sliced seeded halved cucumber
¼ cup	thinly sliced pitted peeled firm mango
1 tbsp	finely chopped peanuts, toasted
2 tsp	lime juice
1 tsp	each fish sauce and vegetable oil
½ tsp	finely minced red finger chili or jalapeño pepper
12	round (9-inch/23 cm) rice paper wrappers
¾ cup	chopped romaine lettuce (about 4 leaves)

How to make it

DIPPING SAUCE: Stir together chili sauce, vinegar, fish sauce and 2 tbsp water; set aside.

RICE PAPER ROLLS: Fill deep Dutch oven with enough salted water to cover lobster when immersed; bring to rolling boil. Grasp back of lobster; plunge headfirst into water. Cook until bright red and small leg comes away easily when twisted and pulled, 10 minutes. Let cool.

Place lobster on cutting board; twist off tail. Using chef's knife, cut tail in half lengthwise; remove meat and cut into small pieces. Place meat in bowl. Remove claws from body. With blunt side of knife, crack claws; pull apart shell and remove meat. Cut meat into small pieces and add to bowl; stir in mint, red pepper, cucumber, mango, peanuts, lime juice, fish sauce, oil and chili pepper until combined.

Fill 10-inch (25 cm) pie plate with lukewarm water; soak 1 rice paper wrapper until pliable, 30 to 60 seconds. Transfer to tea towel; pat dry. Place 4 tsp of the lobster mixture and 1 tbsp of the lettuce at bottom of wrapper. Folding sides over filling, tightly roll up. Repeat with remaining wrappers, lobster mixture and lettuce. *(Make-ahead: Place on plastic wrap–lined plate and cover with damp towel; overwrap with plastic wrap and refrigerate for up to 4 hours.)*

Cut Rice Paper Rolls in half. Serve with Dipping Sauce.

TIP FROM THE TEST KITCHEN

A freshly cooked lobster has the best flavour for these rolls. If you're short on time or don't want to cook one yourself, many fish markets will steam a lobster for you.

NUTRITIONAL INFORMATION, PER PIECE: about 28 cal, 2 g pro, 1 g total fat (trace sat. fat), 4 g carb, trace fibre, 4 mg chol, 102 mg sodium, 40 mg potassium. % RDI: 1% calcium, 1% iron, 2% vit A, 8% vit C, 4% folate.

Chili Cheese Crab Dip

HANDS-ON TIME	TOTAL TIME	MAKES
25 MINUTES	35 MINUTES	ABOUT 2½ CUPS

What you need

2 tbsp	butter
2	shallots, thinly sliced
2	each red finger chili peppers and cloves garlic, minced
2 tbsp	all-purpose flour
1 cup	milk
125 g	cream cheese, cubed and softened
1½ cups	shredded old white Cheddar cheese
1	tub (227 g) crab claw meat, drained
⅓ cup	chopped fresh parsley
1 tbsp	Dijon mustard
pinch	each salt and pepper

How to make it

In saucepan, melt butter over medium heat; cook shallots, chili peppers and garlic, stirring, until softened, about 3 minutes. Sprinkle with flour; cook, stirring, for 2 minutes. Gradually whisk in milk until smooth. Cook, stirring, until thickened, about 4 minutes. Whisk in cream cheese until smooth, about 3 minutes. Whisk in two-thirds of the Cheddar until melted and smooth, about 2 minutes.

Pat crabmeat dry; stir into saucepan along with parsley, mustard, salt and pepper. Scrape into 3-cup (750 mL) ovenproof dish. (*Make-ahead: Let cool for 30 minutes. Cover with foil; refrigerate for up to 24 hours. Reheat, covered, in 400°F/200°C oven for 25 minutes. Uncover and continue with recipe.*)

Sprinkle with remaining Cheddar. Broil until golden and bubbly, 4 minutes. Let stand for 5 minutes before serving.

NUTRITIONAL INFORMATION, PER 1 TBSP: about 43 cal, 2 g pro, 3 g total fat (2 g sat. fat), 1 g carb, trace fibre, 14 mg chol, 84 mg sodium, 34 mg potassium. % RDI: 4% calcium, 2% iron, 5% vit A, 5% vit C, 2% folate.

Smoked Salmon and Artichoke Dip

HANDS-ON TIME	TOTAL TIME	MAKES
5 MINUTES	5 MINUTES	ABOUT 1½ CUPS

What you need

100 g	smoked salmon
½ cup	canned water-packed artichoke hearts, drained
¼ cup	diced red onion
¼ cup	light mayonnaise
¼ cup	light sour cream
1 tbsp	capers, drained
1 tsp	Dijon mustard
½ tsp	grated lemon zest
¼ tsp	pepper
¼ cup	finely chopped fresh chives

How to make it

In food processor, pulse together salmon, artichoke hearts, red onion, mayonnaise, sour cream, capers, mustard, lemon zest and pepper until blended yet still chunky.

Stir in chives. Scrape into serving bowl. (*Make-ahead: Cover and refrigerate for up to 3 days.*)

NUTRITIONAL INFORMATION, PER 1 TBSP: about 19 cal, 1 g pro, 1 g total fat (trace sat. fat), 1 g carb, trace fibre, 2 mg chol, 77 mg sodium, 31 mg potassium. % RDI: 1% calcium, 1% iron, 1% vit A, 2% vit C, 1% folate.

Double Salmon Spread

HANDS-ON TIME	•	TOTAL TIME	•	MAKES
15 MINUTES		1¼ HOURS		ABOUT 2 CUPS

What you need

2	cans (each 213 g) sockeye salmon, drained
⅓ cup	butter, softened
1 tbsp	olive oil
1	pkg (85 g) smoked salmon, diced
2 tbsp	chopped fresh chives
2 tbsp	lemon juice
1 tbsp	chopped drained capers
¼ tsp	sweet paprika

How to make it

Remove and discard skin and bones from canned salmon; place in large bowl and flake with fork.

In small bowl and using fork, mash butter with oil until smooth; fold into salmon. Fold in smoked salmon, chives, lemon juice, capers and paprika. Cover and refrigerate for 1 hour. *(Make-ahead: Refrigerate for up to 24 hours.)*

TIP FROM THE TEST KITCHEN
To soften butter quickly, simply cut it into small cubes and let it stand in a warm place, such as on the stove while the oven is preheating or atop a bowl of warm water.

NUTRITIONAL INFORMATION, PER 1 TBSP: about 42 cal, 3 g pro, 3 g total fat (2 g sat. fat), trace carb, 0 g fibre, 10 mg chol, 81 mg sodium, 39 mg potassium. % RDI: 2% calcium, 1% iron, 2% vit A, 2% vit C.

Clams Casino

HANDS-ON TIME	•	TOTAL TIME	•	MAKES
30 MINUTES		30 MINUTES		24 PIECES

What you need

24	littleneck clams (about 1 kg)
4	strips bacon, chopped
1	shallot, finely chopped
half	jalapeño pepper, seeded and finely chopped
¼ cup	jarred roasted red peppers, drained and finely chopped
1	small clove garlic, minced
2 tsp	unsalted butter
¼ cup	fresh bread crumbs
2 tbsp	chopped fresh parsley
½ tsp	grated lemon zest
1 tbsp	grated Parmesan cheese
	coarse salt

How to make it

Using stiff brush, scrub clams; discard any that do not close when tapped. In Dutch oven or large heavy-bottomed saucepan, bring clams and 1 cup water to boil. Reduce heat to medium; cover and cook until clams are open, about 10 minutes. Discard any that do not open. Using slotted spoon, transfer clams to bowl; discard cooking liquid. Remove and discard top halves of shells. Set clams in half shells aside.

While clams are cooking, in nonstick skillet, cook bacon over medium heat, stirring often, until crisp, about 5 minutes. Using slotted spoon, transfer to paper towel–lined plate; let drain. Set aside.

Reserving 1 tsp fat, drain off and discard remaining fat from skillet; heat reserved fat over medium heat. Cook shallot and jalapeño pepper, stirring often, until shallot is softened, about 4 minutes. Add red peppers and garlic; cook, stirring, until garlic is fragrant, about 1 minute. Stir in bacon. Set aside.

In small nonstick skillet, melt butter over medium heat; cook bread crumbs, stirring occasionally, until light golden, about 3 minutes. Add 1 tbsp of the parsley and the lemon zest; cook, stirring, until fragrant, about 1 minute. Transfer to small bowl; stir in Parmesan.

Fill large rimmed baking sheet with enough coarse salt to cover bottom. Arrange clams, shell side down, in salt to stabilize. Spoon scant 1 tsp of the bacon mixture into each; sprinkle each with scant ½ tsp of the bread crumb mixture. *(Make-ahead: Refrigerate for up to 4 hours.)* Broil until topping is golden, about 2 minutes. Sprinkle with remaining parsley.

NUTRITIONAL INFORMATION, PER PIECE: about 28 cal, 3 g pro, 1 g total fat (trace sat. fat), 1 g carb, trace fibre, 9 mg chol, 53 mg sodium, 75 mg potassium. % RDI: 1% calcium, 19% iron, 3% vit A, 10% vit C, 2% folate.

Smaller Manila clams make a fine substitute for littlenecks. Simply buy more and spoon less of the filling into each.

Lemon-Oregano Shrimp With Creamy Feta Dip

HANDS-ON TIME	•	TOTAL TIME	•	MAKES
15 MINUTES		15 MINUTES		6 TO 8 SERVINGS

What you need

CREAMY FETA DIP:

1 cup	crumbled feta cheese
1	small clove garlic, minced
⅔ cup	light sour cream
⅓ cup	light mayonnaise
¼ tsp	grated lemon zest
2 tsp	lemon juice
1 tbsp	chopped fresh chives

LEMON-OREGANO SHRIMP:

2 tsp	olive oil
2	cloves garlic, minced
¼ tsp	Italian herb seasoning
450 g	large shrimp (31 to 40 count), peeled and deveined
pinch	salt
1 tbsp	fresh oregano leaves, chopped
2 tsp	lemon juice

How to make it

CREAMY FETA DIP: In food processor, purée feta with garlic until smooth. Add sour cream, mayonnaise, lemon zest and lemon juice; purée until smooth. Spoon into serving bowl; stir in chives. Set aside.

LEMON-OREGANO SHRIMP: In large nonstick skillet, heat oil over medium heat; cook garlic and Italian seasoning, stirring often, until fragrant, about 1 minute. Add shrimp and salt; cook, stirring occasionally, until shrimp are pink and opaque throughout, about 4 minutes. Stir in oregano and lemon juice. Serve with Creamy Feta Dip.

TIP FROM THE TEST KITCHEN
This dip is tasty served with toasted pita wedges, crackers or fresh vegetables as well.

NUTRITIONAL INFORMATION, PER EACH OF 8 SERVINGS:
about 174 cal, 13 g pro, 12 g total fat (5 g sat. fat), 4 g carb, trace fibre, 100 mg chol, 362 mg sodium, 160 mg potassium. % RDI: 14% calcium, 10% iron, 7% vit A, 5% vit C, 6% folate.

Salmon Escabeche

HANDS-ON TIME	•	TOTAL TIME	•	MAKES
15 MINUTES		8½ HOURS		6 TO 8 SERVINGS

What you need

750 g	skinless salmon fillet, cut in ¾-inch (2 cm) cubes
1 tbsp	coarse salt
1 tbsp	coarsely ground black pepper
1 tbsp	chopped fresh thyme
1 tsp	smoked paprika
1	onion, finely chopped
1 cup	olive oil
1 cup	dry white wine
1 cup	white wine vinegar

How to make it

Arrange salmon cubes in single layer in 13- x 9-inch (3 L) baking dish; sprinkle all over with salt, pepper, thyme and paprika. Top with onion.

In small saucepan, bring oil, wine and vinegar to boil; drizzle over salmon. Let stand for 20 minutes. Cover with plastic wrap and refrigerate for 8 hours. *(Make-ahead: Refrigerate for up to 2 days.)*

Using slotted spoon, remove salmon from oil mixture. Serve cold or at room temperature.

NUTRITIONAL INFORMATION, PER EACH OF 8 SERVINGS:
about 217 cal, 19 g pro, 14 g total fat (3 g sat. fat), 2 g carb, 1 g fibre, 55 mg chol, 398 mg sodium, 377 mg potassium. % RDI: 2% calcium, 5% iron, 2% vit A, 8% vit C, 12% folate.

Ask your fishmonger for the freshest sushi-grade fish to give this dish the best flavour and texture.

Crispy Calamari

HANDS-ON TIME	•	TOTAL TIME	•	MAKES
35 MINUTES		35 MINUTES		6 SERVINGS

What you need

675 g	whole squid
8 cups	canola, safflower or other vegetable oil
½ cup	all-purpose flour
¼ cup	cornstarch
½ tsp	cayenne pepper
½ tsp	sea salt or salt
1	lemon, cut in wedges

How to make it

Holding each squid tube, pull off head and tentacles; set aside. Rinse tubes under cold water, rubbing off purplish skin. Pull out and discard "pen" (clear long plastic-like skeleton) from centre of each tube. Pull off and discard fins from each tube.

Cut off and discard eyes and head from tentacles, keeping tentacles attached to ring on top; squeeze hard beak from centre of tentacles and discard. Cut tubes crosswise into ½-inch (1 cm) wide rings; pat dry. Pour oil into wok or deep heavy-bottomed saucepan; heat until deep-fryer thermometer reads 375°F (190°C).

Meanwhile, in large plastic bag, shake together flour, cornstarch and cayenne pepper. Add tentacles and rings to flour mixture; shake to coat. Transfer to fine-mesh sieve; lightly shake off excess flour mixture.

Working in batches, fry calamari until golden, 1 to 1½ minutes per batch. Using slotted spoon, transfer to paper towel–lined plate; let drain. Sprinkle with salt; serve with lemon wedges.

TIP FROM THE TEST KITCHEN

Serve the calamari with your favourite sauce, or try our easy basil aïoli: In a food processor, pulse together ¼ cup lightly packed fresh basil leaves; 1 clove garlic, minced or pressed; 2 tbsp extra-virgin olive oil; 2 tsp lemon juice; and 1 tsp anchovy paste until smooth. Blend in ½ cup mayonnaise.

NUTRITIONAL INFORMATION, PER SERVING: about 326 cal, 19 g pro, 20 g total fat (2 g sat. fat), 17 g carb, trace fibre, 265 mg chol, 180 mg sodium. % RDI: 4% calcium, 9% iron, 1% vit C, 12% folate.

Classic Bouillabaisse

HANDS-ON TIME	•	TOTAL TIME	•	MAKES
45 MINUTES		1¾ HOURS		6 SERVINGS

What you need

SEAFOOD STOCK:

450 g	jumbo shrimp (21 to 24 count)
1 tsp	olive oil
1	leek (white and light green parts only), sliced
2	bottles (each 240 mL) clam juice
2	bay leaves

HERBED ROUILLE:

3 tbsp	dry white wine
1 cup	chopped baguette
3 tbsp	each chopped fresh tarragon and olive oil
half	red finger chili pepper, seeded
1 tbsp	light mayonnaise
1	clove garlic

BOUILLABAISSE:

1 tbsp	olive oil
2	cloves garlic, minced
half	bulb fennel, cored and thinly sliced
1	leek (white and light green parts only), sliced
1 tbsp	each tomato paste and grated orange zest
1 cup	dry white wine
½ cup	bottled strained tomatoes (passata)
½ tsp	saffron threads
¼ tsp	each salt and pepper
800 g	littleneck clams (about 12)
250 g	jumbo sea scallops (about 6)
450 g	skinless firm white fish fillets (such as cod or halibut), cut in 1½-inch (4 cm) chunks
¼ cup	chopped fresh parsley

NUTRITIONAL INFORMATION, PER SERVING: about
338 cal, 38 g pro, 14 g total fat (2 g sat. fat), 12 g carb, 2 g fibre,
139 mg chol, 583 mg sodium, 1,008 mg potassium. % RDI:
12% calcium, 46% iron, 13% vit A, 32% vit C, 19% folate.

How to make it

SEAFOOD STOCK: Reserving shells and leaving tails on, peel and devein shrimp; cover and refrigerate shrimp. In food processor, chop shrimp shells. In large heavy-bottomed saucepan, heat oil over medium-high heat; sauté shells and leek until shells are pink, 2 minutes. Add clam juice, bay leaves and 6 cups water; bring to boil. Reduce heat, cover and simmer for 25 minutes, skimming off any foam. Strain through cheesecloth-lined fine-mesh sieve into large bowl, pressing solids to extract liquid; discard solids. Reserve ¼ cup for Herbed Rouille; set remainder aside. (*Make-ahead: Let cool for 30 minutes; refrigerate in airtight container for up to 24 hours.*)

HERBED ROUILLE: Drizzle wine over baguette; let stand for 5 minutes. In food processor, purée reserved Seafood Stock, baguette, tarragon, oil, chili pepper, mayonnaise and garlic until smooth. Refrigerate until ready to use.

BOUILLABAISSE: While stock is simmering, in large saucepan, heat oil over medium heat; cook garlic, stirring, until fragrant, 1 minute. Add fennel and leek; cook, stirring, until slightly softened, 5 minutes. Stir in tomato paste and orange zest; cook over medium-high heat, stirring, until fragrant, 1 minute. Stir in wine; cook for 1 minute. Add remaining Seafood Stock, tomatoes, saffron, salt and pepper; bring to boil. Reduce heat, cover and simmer just until fennel is softened, 30 minutes.

While tomato mixture is cooking, scrub clams; discard any that do not close. Add to pan; cover and cook over medium-high heat for 3 minutes. Add scallops; cook until opaque throughout and clams are open, 3 minutes. Discard any clams that do not open. Using slotted spoon, divide scallops and clams among serving bowls.

Add fish and shrimp to tomato mixture; cook until shrimp are pink and opaque throughout and fish flakes easily when tested, 2 minutes. Using slotted spoon, add fish and shrimp to serving bowls; pour tomato mixture over top. Top with Herbed Rouille; sprinkle with parsley.

Tomato Shrimp Soup

HANDS-ON TIME	•	TOTAL TIME	•	MAKES
1 HOUR		1¾ HOURS		6 SERVINGS

What you need

1	head garlic
900 g	ripe tomatoes
1	large white onion, quartered
3 tbsp	olive oil
450 g	large shrimp (31 to 40 count)
1	serrano or jalapeño pepper, seeded and chopped
1 cup	coarsely chopped fresh cilantro stems and leaves
1	rib celery with leaves, chopped
2	cloves garlic, minced
1	dried or canned chipotle pepper, split lengthwise and seeded
½ tsp	ground cumin
¼ tsp	pepper
1	bottle (240 mL) clam juice
1 tsp	dried oregano
1 tsp	salt
2 tbsp	lime juice
	fresh cilantro leaves

How to make it

Slice garlic head in half crosswise. In roasting pan, toss together garlic halves, tomatoes, onion and 1 tbsp of the oil. Roast in 450°F (230°C) oven, turning onion and garlic halfway through, for 40 minutes. Let cool slightly; squeeze garlic cloves into blender. Scrape tomato mixture into blender. Pour 1 cup water into roasting pan; using wooden spoon, stir and scrape up browned bits. Pour into blender; purée until smooth.

While garlic mixture is roasting, reserving shells, peel and devein shrimp; slice each in half lengthwise. Refrigerate shrimp until needed.

In large saucepan, heat remaining oil over medium-high heat; sauté serrano pepper, chopped cilantro, celery, garlic, chipotle pepper, cumin and pepper for 3 minutes. Stir in shrimp shells; sauté until shells are pink.

Stir in clam juice, roasted garlic mixture, oregano, salt and 3 cups water; bring to boil. Reduce heat to low; cover and simmer for 30 minutes. Strain through fine-mesh sieve into clean saucepan, pressing solids to extract liquid. Discard solids.

Bring soup to boil; add shrimp and return to boil. Reduce heat, cover and simmer until shrimp are pink and opaque throughout, about 3 minutes. Stir in lime juice.

Divide among serving bowls; garnish with cilantro.

TIP FROM THE TEST KITCHEN
To make an even spicier soup, use up to three serrano peppers and up to two chipotle peppers.

NUTRITIONAL INFORMATION, PER SERVING: about 179 cal, 14 g pro, 8 g total fat (1 g sat. fat), 12 g carb, trace fibre, 87 mg chol, 572 mg sodium, 681 mg potassium. % RDI: 8% calcium, 19% iron, 21% vit A, 40% vit C, 14% folate.

Cioppino

HANDS-ON TIME	TOTAL TIME	MAKES
20 MINUTES	30 MINUTES	4 SERVINGS

What you need

1 tbsp	olive oil
1	small sweet onion, diced
4	cloves garlic, minced
¼ cup	dry white wine
1 cup	bottled strained tomatoes (passata)
1 tsp	dried oregano
¼ tsp	pepper
1	bottle (240 mL) clam juice
225 g	jumbo shrimp (21 to 24 count), peeled and deveined
225 g	jumbo sea scallops (see tip, below)
225 g	skinless firm white fish fillet (such as cod or halibut), cut crosswise in strips

How to make it

In large saucepan, heat oil over medium-high heat; cook onion, stirring occasionally, until softened, about 4 minutes. Add garlic; cook, stirring, for 1 minute.

Pour in wine; cook, scraping up browned bits, until liquid is slightly reduced, about 1 minute. Add tomatoes, oregano, pepper and clam juice; bring to boil. Reduce heat and simmer for 5 minutes.

Stir in shrimp, scallops and fish; cover and cook over medium heat until shrimp are pink, and fish and scallops are opaque throughout, about 5 minutes.

TIP FROM THE TEST KITCHEN
If your scallops are more than 1 inch (2.5 cm) thick, halve them horizontally to ensure they cook in the same amount of time as the shrimp and fish.

NUTRITIONAL INFORMATION, PER SERVING: about 219 cal, 29 g pro, 5 g total fat (1 g sat. fat), 11 g carb, 1 g fibre, 109 mg chol, 438 mg sodium, 801 mg potassium. % RDI: 7% calcium, 22% iron, 4% vit A, 13% vit C, 13% folate.

Shrimp and Fish Chowder

HANDS-ON TIME	**TOTAL TIME**	**MAKES**
15 MINUTES	30 MINUTES	4 SERVINGS

What you need

1	sheet (half 450 g pkg) frozen butter puff pastry, thawed
1	egg, lightly beaten
2 tbsp	butter
1	leek (white and light green parts only), thinly sliced
2 tbsp	all-purpose flour
1 cup	sodium-reduced chicken broth
½ cup	clam juice
½ cup	10% cream
450 g	large shrimp (31 to 40 count), peeled and deveined
300 g	skinless cod or other firm white fish fillets, cut in 1-inch (2.5 cm) pieces
1 tbsp	chopped fresh tarragon (or ½ tsp dried)
½ tsp	grated lemon zest
2 tbsp	lemon juice
¼ tsp	pepper

How to make it

Cut pastry into quarters; cut each in half to form 8 triangles. Place on parchment paper–lined rimmed baking sheet; brush with egg. Bake in 400°F (200°C) oven until puffed and golden, 18 to 20 minutes.

While pastry is baking, in large saucepan, melt butter over medium heat; cook leek, stirring occasionally, until softened, about 4 minutes. Add flour; cook, stirring, for 1 minute. Stir in broth, clam juice and cream; cook, stirring, until slightly thickened, 2 to 3 minutes.

Stir in shrimp, fish, tarragon, lemon zest, lemon juice and pepper; cook over medium-high heat until shrimp are pink and fish is opaque throughout, 5 to 6 minutes.

Divide soup among serving bowls; serve with puff pastry.

TIP FROM THE TEST KITCHEN
In a hurry? Skip the puff pastry and serve the chowder with crusty bread instead.

NUTRITIONAL INFORMATION, PER SERVING: about 561 cal, 39 g pro, 31 g total fat (9 g sat. fat), 31 g carb, 1 g fibre, 234 mg chol, 574 mg sodium, 645 mg potassium. % RDI: 11% calcium, 31% iron, 14% vit A, 13% vit C, 27% folate.

Chilled Dill and Cucumber Soup With Salmon Crostini

HANDS-ON TIME 25 MINUTES	•	**TOTAL TIME** 1½ HOURS	•	**MAKES** 4 SERVINGS

What you need

3	English cucumbers, chopped
1	clove garlic, halved
2 cups	2% plain yogurt
3 tbsp	chopped fresh dill
1 tbsp	lemon juice
½ tsp	each salt and pepper
12	slices (¼ inch/5 mm thick) baguette
100 g	sliced smoked salmon
4	radishes, thinly sliced

How to make it

In blender, purée together 8 cups of the cucumbers, the garlic, 1½ cups of the yogurt, 2 tbsp of the dill, the lemon juice, salt and pepper until smooth. Cover and refrigerate for 1 hour. *(Make-ahead: Refrigerate for up to 24 hours.)*

Meanwhile, arrange baguette slices on parchment paper–lined rimmed baking sheet; bake in 400°F (200°C) oven until crisp and light golden, about 6 minutes. *(Make-ahead: Store in airtight container for up to 24 hours.)*

Top baguette slices with salmon and remaining dill. Divide soup among serving bowls; drizzle remaining yogurt over soup. Top with radishes and remaining chopped cucumber.

TIP FROM THE TEST KITCHEN
This is a delicious soup to make ahead. Chilling helps develop the subtle flavours of the ingredients.

NUTRITIONAL INFORMATION, PER SERVING: about 180 cal, 13 g pro, 4 g total fat (2 g sat. fat), 24 g carb, 2 g fibre, 17 mg chol, 655 mg sodium, 675 mg potassium. % RDI: 22% calcium, 11% iron, 6% vit A, 17% vit C, 17% folate.

Easy Bouillabaisse

HANDS-ON TIME	TOTAL TIME	MAKES
20 MINUTES	35 MINUTES	4 SERVINGS

What you need

1 tbsp	each olive oil and butter
½ cup	finely chopped shallots or onion
1	bay leaf
2	plum tomatoes, seeded and chopped
1	clove garlic, minced
¼ tsp	salt
1	bottle (240 mL) clam juice
½ cup	dry white wine or water
450 g	mussels, scrubbed (see tip, below)
225 g	skinless halibut or cod fillets, cubed
2 tbsp	chopped fresh parsley

How to make it

In large saucepan, heat oil and butter over medium heat; cook shallots and bay leaf, stirring often, until shallots are softened, about 3 minutes.

Stir in tomatoes, garlic and salt; cook, stirring, for 1 minute. Stir in clam juice, wine and 1 cup water; bring to boil. Reduce heat, cover and simmer for 10 minutes.

Add mussels and fish; cover and cook until mussels open and fish flakes easily when tested, about 6 minutes. Discard bay leaf and any mussels that do not open. Stir in parsley.

NUTRITIONAL INFORMATION, PER SERVING: about 178 cal, 17 g pro, 8 g total fat (3 g sat. fat), 6 g carb, 1 g fibre, 37 mg chol, 395 mg sodium, 563 mg potassium. % RDI: 5% calcium, 17% iron, 13% vit A, 15% vit C, 14% folate.

Seafood and Fennel Soup

HANDS-ON TIME	TOTAL TIME	MAKES
30 MINUTES	30 MINUTES	4 TO 6 SERVINGS

What you need

1 tbsp	olive oil
2	leeks (white and light green parts only), halved lengthwise and thinly sliced crosswise
3	cloves garlic, minced
1	bulb fennel, cored and thinly sliced
1	bottle (240 mL) clam juice
¾ tsp	salt
pinch	pepper
12	jumbo sea scallops (250 g)
250 g	wild haddock or cod fillet, cut in 1-inch (2.5 cm) chunks
1	parsnip or yellow carrot, thinly sliced (see tip, below)
2 tbsp	lemon juice
1 tbsp	each chopped fresh dill and fresh tarragon

How to make it

In Dutch oven or large heavy-bottomed saucepan, heat oil over medium heat; cook leeks and garlic, stirring occasionally, until softened, about 5 minutes. Add fennel; cook, stirring, just until softened, about 3 minutes.

Stir in clam juice, salt, pepper and 4 cups water; bring to boil. Reduce heat to gentle simmer; cover and cook until fennel is tender, about 4 minutes.

Increase heat to medium. Stir in scallops; cook just until opaque throughout, about 1 minute. Stir in fish, parsnip and lemon juice; cook, uncovered and without stirring, until fish is opaque throughout, about 2 minutes.

Divide soup among serving bowls; sprinkle with dill and tarragon.

TIP FROM THE TEST KITCHEN
To keep cooking time to a minimum, slice the parsnip as thinly as you can.

NUTRITIONAL INFORMATION, PER EACH OF 6 SERVINGS:
about 146 cal, 17 g pro, 3 g total fat (1 g sat. fat), 14 g carb, 3 g fibre, 39 mg chol, 504 mg sodium, 653 mg potassium. % RDI: 8% calcium, 13% iron, 7% vit A, 22% vit C, 21% folate.

Orange Salmon and Orzo Salad

HANDS-ON TIME	•	TOTAL TIME	•	MAKES
25 MINUTES		30 MINUTES		4 SERVINGS

What you need

ORANGE-CHIVE DRESSING:

½ tsp	grated orange zest
3 tbsp	orange juice
2 tbsp	chopped fresh chives
2 tsp	Dijon mustard
1 tsp	liquid honey
1	clove garlic, finely grated or pressed
½ tsp	each salt and pepper
⅓ cup	vegetable oil

SALAD:

450 g	skinless salmon fillet
pinch	each salt and pepper
¼ cup	chopped fresh parsley
4 tsp	Dijon mustard
2 tsp	grated orange zest (see tip, below)
1½ cups	orzo
2 cups	snow peas, trimmed and sliced diagonally
8 cups	baby arugula
2 cups	watercress or living cress leaves (see tip, opposite)

How to make it

ORANGE-CHIVE DRESSING: In small bowl, whisk together orange zest, orange juice, chives, mustard, honey, garlic, salt and pepper. Gradually drizzle in oil, whisking until emulsified. Set aside.

SALAD: Place fish on lightly greased foil-lined rimmed baking sheet; sprinkle with salt and pepper. Stir together parsley, mustard and orange zest; spread over fish. Bake in 400°F (200°C) oven until fish flakes easily when tested, about 15 minutes. Transfer to cutting board; chop or break into large chunks.

While fish is baking, in large saucepan of boiling salted water, cook orzo for 30 seconds less than package instructions for al dente. Add snow peas; cook until orzo is al dente and peas are bright green and tender-crisp, about 30 seconds. Drain.

In large bowl, toss together orzo mixture, arugula, watercress and Orange-Chive Dressing. Gently fold in fish.

TIP FROM THE TEST KITCHEN
Apply gentle pressure when zesting citrus. You want to grate just the surface of the rind; if you press too hard, you'll get too much of the bitter white pith.

NUTRITIONAL INFORMATION, PER SERVING: about 635 cal, 32 g pro, 31 g total fat (4 g sat. fat), 56 g carb, 4 g fibre, 55 mg chol, 714 mg sodium, 721 mg potassium. % RDI: 11% calcium, 21% iron, 20% vit A, 75% vit C, 43% folate.

Thai Crab Cake Salad With Red Curry Mayo

HANDS-ON TIME
30 MINUTES

TOTAL TIME
30 MINUTES

MAKES
4 TO 6 SERVINGS

What you need

CRAB CAKES:

1	tub (454 g) crab claw meat, drained and coarsely chopped
¼ cup	chopped fresh cilantro
¼ cup	dried bread crumbs
2	green onions, chopped
1	egg, lightly beaten
1 tbsp	Thai red curry paste
1 tbsp	vegetable oil

RED CURRY MAYO:

3 tbsp	light mayonnaise
1 tsp	Thai red curry paste

LIME VINAIGRETTE:

2 tbsp	lime juice
1	clove garlic, finely grated or pressed
1 tsp	grated fresh ginger
1 tsp	liquid honey
pinch	each salt and pepper
¼ cup	vegetable oil

SALAD:

12 cups	lightly packed baby spinach
2 cups	lightly packed watercress or living cress leaves (about 1 bunch), see tip, right
2	avocados, pitted, peeled and diced
1	sweet red pepper, diced

How to make it

CRAB CAKES: Stir together crabmeat, cilantro, bread crumbs, green onions, egg and curry paste until well combined. Shape into twelve ¾-inch (2 cm) thick patties. *(Make-ahead: Cover and refrigerate for up to 24 hours.)*

In large nonstick skillet, heat oil over medium heat. Working in batches, cook crab cakes, turning once, until firm and golden, about 6 minutes per batch. Transfer to plate; keep warm.

RED CURRY MAYO: While crab cakes are cooking, whisk mayonnaise with curry paste. Set aside. *(Make-ahead: Cover and refrigerate for up to 2 days.)*

LIME VINAIGRETTE: In large bowl, whisk together lime juice, garlic, ginger, honey, salt and pepper. Gradually drizzle in oil, whisking until emulsified.

SALAD: Add spinach, watercress, avocados and red pepper to Lime Vinaigrette; toss to combine. To serve, top with Crab Cakes and Red Curry Mayo.

TIP FROM THE TEST KITCHEN
Living cress is also known as garden cress. These small sprouts are a relative of watercress and have a similar peppery flavour. You'll find packages of living cress where other fresh sprouts are sold.

NUTRITIONAL INFORMATION, PER EACH OF 6 SERVINGS:
about 329 cal, 16 g pro, 24 g total fat (3 g sat. fat), 14 g carb, 5 g fibre, 87 mg chol, 676 mg sodium, 741 mg potassium. % RDI: 11% calcium, 27% iron, 64% vit A, 102% vit C, 73% folate.

Crispy Mackerel
With Pancetta and Herbed Salad

HANDS-ON TIME	TOTAL TIME	MAKES
25 MINUTES	25 MINUTES	4 SERVINGS

What you need

How to make it

CRISPY MACKEREL:

4	thin slices pancetta (about 30 g), coarsely chopped
½ cup	all-purpose flour
4	skin-on wild mackerel fillets (each about 115 g), pin bones removed (see tip, below)
pinch	each salt and pepper
2 tbsp	butter

HERBED SALAD:

4 tsp	extra-virgin olive oil
2 tsp	balsamic vinegar
pinch	each salt and pepper
4 cups	lightly packed mixed baby greens
1 cup	grape or cherry tomatoes, halved
¼ cup	fresh tarragon leaves
¼ cup	fresh basil leaves, torn
1 tbsp	chopped fresh chives
	lemon wedges

CRISPY MACKEREL: In large nonstick skillet, cook pancetta over medium heat, stirring often, until crisp, 5 minutes. Using slotted spoon, transfer to paper towel–lined plate; let drain. Drain fat into small bowl; set aside.

Sprinkle flour in shallow dish. Using sharp knife, score fish skin to make crosshatch pattern. Sprinkle fish with salt and pepper; dredge in flour, turning to generously coat both sides.

In same skillet, heat half each of the reserved fat and butter over medium heat; add half of the fish, skin side down; cook for 4 minutes. Turn; cook until fish flakes easily when tested, about 1 minute. Wipe out skillet; repeat with remaining fat, butter and fish.

HERBED SALAD: While fish is cooking, in large bowl, whisk together oil, vinegar, salt and pepper; add greens, tomatoes, tarragon and basil. Toss to coat.

TO FINISH: Divide Herbed Salad among serving plates. Top with Crispy Mackerel, pancetta and chives. Serve with lemon wedges.

TIP FROM THE TEST KITCHEN

Use clean, sharp tweezers or needle-nose pliers to remove the pin bones from the flesh of the fish. Pull them out firmly but gently, working at the same angle as the bones to keep the flesh from tearing.

NUTRITIONAL INFORMATION, PER SERVING: about 363 cal, 25 g pro, 26 g total fat (7 g sat. fat), 7 g carb, 2 g fibre, 83 mg chol, 221 mg sodium, 684 mg potassium. % RDI: 7% calcium, 20% iron, 65% vit A, 25% vit C, 36% folate.

Scoring the fish skin with a
sharp knife keeps it from curling
and makes it extra crispy.

Trout Niçoise Salad

HANDS-ON TIME
20 MINUTES

•

TOTAL TIME
30 MINUTES

•

MAKES
4 SERVINGS

What you need

4	eggs (shell on)
225 g	green beans, trimmed
10	mini yellow-fleshed potatoes
2	skin-on trout fillets (each about 225 g), halved crosswise
¼ tsp	each salt and pepper
⅓ cup	extra-virgin olive oil
¼ cup	lemon juice
2 tsp	finely chopped fresh tarragon
1 tsp	Dijon mustard
1 tsp	liquid honey
4 cups	mixed baby greens
20	Niçoise or other black olives
2	small tomatoes, each cut in 6 wedges

How to make it

Place eggs in saucepan; pour in enough cold water to cover by at least 1 inch (2.5 cm). Cover and bring to boil. Immediately remove from heat; let stand for 12 minutes. Drain eggs; rinse under cold water for 1 minute. Drain; peel off shells. Cut eggs in half lengthwise; set aside

While eggs are cooking, in large saucepan of boiling lightly salted water, cook green beans until tender-crisp, about 1 minute. Using tongs, transfer to bowl of ice water; let cool. Drain well.

Add potatoes to same saucepan of boiling water; cook until tender, about 12 minutes. Drain; cut in half.

Sprinkle fish with half each of the salt and pepper. In large nonstick skillet, heat ½ tsp of the oil over medium-high heat; cook fish, turning once, until fish flakes easily when tested, about 4 minutes.

While fish is cooking, in small bowl, stir together lemon juice, tarragon, mustard, honey, and remaining salt and pepper. Gradually drizzle in remaining oil, whisking until emulsified.

Divide eggs, green beans, potatoes, baby greens, olives and tomatoes among serving plates. Top each with 1 piece of the fish; drizzle with dressing.

TIP FROM THE TEST KITCHEN
If you like, substitute flaked canned tuna for the trout for an even easier meal, and a classic Niçoise salad presentation.

NUTRITIONAL INFORMATION, PER SERVING: about 527 cal, 33 g pro, 35 g total fat (7 g sat. fat), 20 g carb, 3 g fibre, 251 mg chol, 690 mg sodium, 1,039 mg potassium. % RDI: 16% calcium, 17% iron, 34% vit A, 52% vit C, 55% folate.

Tuna and Potato Salad
With Lemon-Caper Dressing

HANDS-ON TIME	TOTAL TIME	MAKES
20 MINUTES	30 MINUTES	4 SERVINGS

What you need

How to make it

LEMON-CAPER DRESSING:

3 tbsp	lemon juice
4 tsp	chopped drained capers
1 tbsp	grainy mustard
2 tsp	liquid honey
½ tsp	each salt and pepper
⅓ cup	olive oil

SALAD:

690 g	mini red-skinned potatoes
8 cups	sliced or torn Little Gem or romaine lettuce
150 g	oil-packed solid light albacore tuna (see tip, below), drained and broken in chunks
1 cup	shredded radicchio
2	shallots, thinly sliced

LEMON-CAPER DRESSING: In small bowl, whisk together lemon juice, capers, mustard, honey, salt and pepper. Gradually drizzle in oil, whisking until emulsified. Set aside.

SALAD: In large saucepan of boiling salted water, cook potatoes until fork-tender, about 10 minutes. Drain; let cool for 10 minutes. Cut in half.

In large bowl, gently toss together potatoes, lettuce, tuna, radicchio, shallots and Lemon-Caper Dressing.

TIP FROM THE TEST KITCHEN
Good-quality oil-packed tuna has more moisture and flavour than water-packed, but either will work in this recipe.

NUTRITIONAL INFORMATION, PER SERVING: about 379 cal, 12 g pro, 21 g total fat (3 g sat. fat), 39 g carb, 6 g fibre, 7 mg chol, 991 mg sodium, 1,157 mg potassium. % RDI: 6% calcium, 21% iron, 85% vit A, 90% vit C, 78% folate.

Scallop, Sweet Pepper and Zucchini Salad

HANDS-ON TIME
15 MINUTES

•

TOTAL TIME
15 MINUTES

•

MAKES
4 SERVINGS

What you need

¼ cup	extra-virgin olive oil
2 tbsp	red wine vinegar
1 tsp	liquid honey
1	small clove garlic, minced
¾ tsp	chopped fresh thyme
¼ tsp	each salt and pepper
1	sweet yellow, red or orange pepper, diced
1	zucchini, diced
half	red onion, diced
450 g	jumbo sea scallops (about 20)
4 cups	packed baby spinach

How to make it

In small bowl, whisk together all but 1 tsp of the oil, the vinegar, honey, garlic, ½ tsp of the thyme and half each of the salt and pepper. Stir in sweet pepper, zucchini and red onion; set aside.

Pat scallops dry with paper towel; sprinkle with remaining thyme, salt and pepper. In large nonstick skillet, heat remaining oil over medium-high heat; cook scallops, turning once, until golden and opaque throughout, about 4 minutes.

Toss spinach with sweet pepper mixture; arrange on serving platter. Top with scallops.

NUTRITIONAL INFORMATION, PER SERVING: about 253 cal, 21 g pro, 15 g total fat (2 g sat. fat), 9 g carb, 2 g fibre, 43 mg chol, 389 mg sodium, 782 mg potassium. % RDI: 13% calcium, 27% iron, 45% vit A, 90% vit C, 46% folate.

Atlantic Shrimp Salad on Rye

HANDS-ON TIME	•	TOTAL TIME	•	MAKES
20 MINUTES		20 MINUTES		4 SERVINGS

What you need

2	pkg (each 340 g) cooked peeled cold-water shrimp (see tip, below)
¼ cup	light mayonnaise
2 tbsp	lemon juice
1 tbsp	each chopped fresh parsley, fresh chives and fresh dill
1	green onion, thinly sliced
¼ tsp	pepper
pinch	salt
8	leaves Boston lettuce
1 cup	thinly sliced radishes
8	slices rye or sourdough bread
30 g	pea sprouts

How to make it

Place shrimp between 2 paper towels and pat dry, gently pressing out any liquid.

In bowl, stir together shrimp, mayonnaise, lemon juice, parsley, chives, dill, green onion, pepper and salt.

Divide lettuce, shrimp mixture and radishes among bread slices. Top with pea sprouts.

TIP FROM THE TEST KITCHEN
Cold-water shrimp are prized for their tenderness and sweet taste; plus, they're the perfect size for salads and sandwich fillings. Choose shrimp that are certified by the Aquaculture Stewardship Council to ensure they're sustainably harvested.

NUTRITIONAL INFORMATION, PER SERVING: about 396 cal, 41 g pro, 10 g total fat (2 g sat. fat), 34 g carb, 5 g fibre, 264 mg chol, 762 mg sodium, 554 mg potassium. % RDI: 14% calcium, 45% iron, 18% vit A, 32% vit C, 43% folate.

Want a lower-carb option?
Double up on the lettuce, skip the
bread and serve as a plated meal.

Avocado Lobster Rolls

HANDS-ON TIME	TOTAL TIME	MAKES
15 MINUTES	15 MINUTES	4 SERVINGS

What you need

2	cooked lobsters (each about 400 g), see tip, below
½ cup	2% plain Greek yogurt
3 tbsp	light mayonnaise
1 tbsp	lemon juice
2 tsp	Dijon mustard
1 tsp	Worcestershire sauce
1	rib celery, diced
half	avocado, pitted, peeled and chopped
4 tsp	chopped fresh tarragon
2	green onions, sliced
4	hotdog buns

How to make it

Place 1 lobster on cutting board; twist off tail. Using sharp chef's knife, cut tail in half lengthwise; remove meat from tail and cut into bite-size chunks. Remove claws from body. With blunt side of knife, crack claws; pull apart shell and remove meat. Cut into bite-size chunks. Repeat with remaining lobster.

In bowl, whisk together yogurt, mayonnaise, lemon juice, mustard and Worcestershire sauce. Stir in lobster, celery, avocado, tarragon and all but 1 tbsp of the green onions.

Spoon lobster mixture into hotdog buns; garnish with remaining green onions.

TIP FROM THE TEST KITCHEN
If you can't find freshly cooked lobsters, substitute 1 can (320 g) frozen cooked lobster meat. Thaw and drain it well before using.

NUTRITIONAL INFORMATION, PER SERVING: about 282 cal, 18 g pro, 11 g total fat (2 g sat. fat), 30 g carb, 3 g fibre, 39 mg chol, 552 mg sodium, 439 mg potassium. % RDI: 13% calcium, 16% iron, 4% vit A, 8% vit C, 39% folate.

Cornmeal-Crusted Pickerel BLT

HANDS-ON TIME	•	TOTAL TIME	•	MAKES
15 MINUTES		15 MINUTES		4 SERVINGS

What you need

CLASSIC TARTAR SAUCE:

⅓ cup	light mayonnaise
2 tbsp	chopped cornichons (see tip, below)
1 tbsp	chopped rinsed drained capers (optional)
1 tsp	lemon juice
pinch	each salt and pepper

SANDWICHES:

4	strips bacon (optional)
4	skinless pickerel fillets (each about 115 g)
¼ tsp	each salt and pepper
⅓ cup	cornmeal
1 tbsp	vegetable oil
4	leaves romaine lettuce
2	plum tomatoes, sliced
4	oval buns, halved

How to make it

CLASSIC TARTAR SAUCE: Mix together mayonnaise, cornichons, capers (if using), lemon juice, salt and pepper. Cover and refrigerate until ready to use.

SANDWICHES: Halve bacon crosswise (if using). In nonstick skillet, cook bacon over medium heat, turning once, until crisp, about 8 minutes. Transfer to paper towel–lined plate; let drain. Drain fat from skillet.

Meanwhile, sprinkle fish with salt and pepper. Place cornmeal in shallow dish; press fish into cornmeal, turning to coat.

In same skillet, heat oil over medium heat; cook fish, turning once, until crisp, golden and fish flakes easily when tested, 6 to 8 minutes.

Sandwich fish, Classic Tartar Sauce, lettuce, tomatoes and bacon in buns.

TIP FROM THE TEST KITCHEN
Cornichons are tiny sour gherkin pickles. If you can't find them or prefer a sweet-tart taste, substitute chopped sweet gherkins or sweet green relish for them.

NUTRITIONAL INFORMATION, PER SERVING: about 425 cal, 29 g pro, 14 g total fat (2 g sat. fat), 44 g carb, 3 g fibre, 104 mg chol, 779 mg sodium, 649 mg potassium. % RDI: 18% calcium, 29% iron, 16% vit A, 13% vit C, 49% folate.

Lemon Herb Shrimp Burgers

HANDS-ON TIME
15 MINUTES

•

TOTAL TIME
20 MINUTES

•

MAKES
4 SERVINGS

What you need

LIGHTENED-UP TARTAR SAUCE:

2 tbsp	each light mayonnaise and plain yogurt
2 tbsp	chopped bread-and-butter pickles
1 tsp	Dijon mustard
1 tsp	lemon juice
pinch	salt
dash	hot pepper sauce

SHRIMP BURGERS:

½ cup	fresh bread crumbs
1	egg
2	cloves garlic, chopped
1 tsp	grated lemon zest
1 tbsp	lemon juice
450 g	large shrimp (31 to 40 count), peeled and deveined
1 tbsp	each chopped fresh parsley, fresh chives and fresh dill
pinch	each salt and pepper
1 tbsp	vegetable oil
1 cup	finely shredded green cabbage
4	soft white buns, halved

How to make it

LIGHTENED-UP TARTAR SAUCE: Whisk together mayonnaise, yogurt, pickles, mustard, lemon juice, salt and hot pepper sauce. Cover and refrigerate until ready to use.

SHRIMP BURGERS: In food processor, pulse together bread crumbs, egg, garlic, lemon zest and lemon juice until combined. Add shrimp; pulse until combined, about 6 times. Stir in parsley, chives, dill, salt and pepper.

In large skillet, heat oil over medium-high heat; divide shrimp mixture into quarters and scoop into skillet, pressing gently to form about ½-inch (1 cm) thick patties. Cook, turning once, until firm and golden, and shrimp is pink and opaque throughout, 6 to 8 minutes.

TO FINISH: Sandwich Shrimp Burgers, cabbage and Lightened-Up Tartar Sauce in buns.

TIP FROM THE TEST KITCHEN

Don't throw out the shrimp shells. Pop them in the freezer and later, when you have time, simmer them in vegetable or chicken broth to extract their flavour. Strain the flavoured broth and use it in fish soups, chowders, stews, savoury pies and pastas.

NUTRITIONAL INFORMATION, PER SERVING: about 338 cal, 25 g pro, 12 g total fat (2 g sat. fat), 33 g carb, 2 g fibre, 179 mg chol, 518 mg sodium, 320 mg potassium. % RDI: 14% calcium, 31% iron, 9% vit A, 20% vit C, 39% folate.

Shredded cabbage gives this savoury
burger a satisfying crunch, but you
can swap it for lettuce if you like.

Fajitas and tacos are
yummy ways to add more
fish to your diet.

Tilapia and Red Pepper Fajitas

HANDS-ON TIME	TOTAL TIME	MAKES
25 MINUTES	25 MINUTES	4 SERVINGS

What you need

½ tsp	each smoked paprika and chili powder
¼ tsp	ground cumin
pinch	each salt and pepper
300 g	skinless tilapia fillets
4 tsp	canola oil
1	onion, thinly sliced
1	sweet red pepper, thinly sliced
1 cup	rinsed drained canned black beans
½ cup	frozen corn kernels
2 tsp	lime juice
8	small soft flour tortillas (6 inches/15 cm), warmed
⅓ cup	chopped fresh cilantro
⅓ cup	sour cream

How to make it

Mix together paprika, chili powder, cumin, salt and pepper; rub all over fish.

In nonstick skillet, heat half of the oil over medium heat; cook fish, turning once, until fish flakes easily when tested, 8 to 10 minutes. Transfer to plate; let cool enough to handle. Break into bite-size pieces.

While fish is cooling, add remaining oil to skillet; cook onion and red pepper over medium heat, stirring occasionally, until onion is softened and golden, about 8 minutes.

Stir in beans and corn; cook, stirring often, until corn is heated through, about 3 minutes. Stir in fish and lime juice. Scrape into serving dish; serve with tortillas, cilantro and sour cream.

VARIATION

Shrimp and Red Pepper Fajitas

Replace tilapia fillets with 300 g large shrimp (31 to 40 count), peeled and deveined. Add shrimp to skillet along with corn. Cook until shrimp are pink and opaque throughout, about 6 minutes.

NUTRITIONAL INFORMATION, PER SERVING: about 395 cal, 25 g pro, 13 g total fat (3 g sat. fat), 47 g carb, 6 g fibre, 44 mg chol, 650 mg sodium, 639 mg potassium. % RDI: 6% calcium, 24% iron, 14% vit A, 88% vit C, 55% folate.

Fish Tacos With Mango-Avocado Salsa

HANDS-ON TIME
20 MINUTES

•

TOTAL TIME
20 MINUTES

•

MAKES
4 SERVINGS

What you need

MANGO SALSA:

½ cup	diced pitted peeled mango
1	avocado, pitted, peeled and diced
⅓ cup	finely chopped red onion
1 tsp	grated lime zest
2 tsp	lime juice
pinch	each salt and pepper

YOGURT SAUCE:

½ cup	Greek yogurt
1 tbsp	lime juice

FISH TACOS:

225 g	skinless tilapia fillets
¼ tsp	ground allspice
pinch	each salt and pepper
⅔ cup	panko bread crumbs
¼ cup	all-purpose flour
1	egg, lightly beaten
1 tbsp	vegetable oil
8	small soft corn tortillas (6 inches/15 cm), warmed

How to make it

MANGO SALSA: Gently stir together mango, avocado, red onion, lime zest, lime juice, salt and pepper. Set aside.

YOGURT SAUCE: Stir yogurt with lime juice. Set aside.

FISH TACOS: Sprinkle fish with allspice, salt and pepper. Place panko, flour and egg in separate shallow dishes. Dredge fish in flour, shaking off excess. Dip into egg, letting excess drip off. Dredge fish in panko, pressing to adhere.

In nonstick skillet, heat oil over medium heat; cook fish, turning once, until golden and fish flakes easily when tested, 6 to 8 minutes. Break into chunks.

Divide fish among tortillas; top with Mango Salsa and Yogurt Sauce.

TIP FROM THE TEST KITCHEN
To give the salsa a spicy kick, add a dash or two of hot pepper sauce made from Scotch bonnet peppers.

NUTRITIONAL INFORMATION, PER SERVING: about 437 cal, 22 g pro, 20 g total fat (5 g sat. fat), 43 g carb, 6 g fibre, 61 mg chol, 363 mg sodium, 580 mg potassium. % RDI: 13% calcium, 14% iron, 4% vit A, 23% vit C, 25% folate.

Shrimp and Bok Choy Lettuce Wraps

HANDS-ON TIME	•	TOTAL TIME	•	MAKES
30 MINUTES		30 MINUTES		4 SERVINGS

What you need

PEANUT-LIME SAUCE:

3 tbsp	smooth natural peanut butter
1 tbsp	lime juice
1 tbsp	sodium-reduced soy sauce
1 tbsp	liquid honey
1	clove garlic, minced
pinch	pepper

LETTUCE WRAPS:

1	large head iceberg lettuce (see tip, below)
2 tsp	vegetable oil
225 g	extra-jumbo shrimp (16 to 20 count), peeled and deveined
2	cloves garlic, minced
1 tsp	minced fresh ginger
2	large heads Shanghai bok choy (about 200 g), thinly sliced
1	carrot, cut in matchsticks
pinch	each salt and pepper
1 cup	bean sprouts
1	green onion, sliced
¼ cup	chopped unsalted peanuts, toasted

How to make it

PEANUT-LIME SAUCE: Whisk together peanut butter, lime juice, soy sauce, honey, garlic, pepper and 2 tbsp water. Set aside.

LETTUCE WRAPS: Halve and core lettuce; gently separate 8 large leaves, trimming if necessary to make 5-inch (12 cm) lettuce cups. Set aside.

In wok or large nonstick skillet, heat half of the oil over medium-high heat; cook shrimp, turning occasionally, until pink and opaque throughout, about 6 minutes. Transfer to cutting board; halve lengthwise. Set aside.

In same skillet, heat remaining oil over medium heat; cook garlic and ginger, stirring, until fragrant, about 20 seconds. Add bok choy, carrot, salt and pepper; cook, stirring, until tender-crisp, about 2 minutes. Stir in bean sprouts, green onion and shrimp.

Spoon shrimp mixture into lettuce cups. Drizzle with Peanut-Lime Sauce; sprinkle with peanuts.

TIP FROM THE TEST KITCHEN

Choose the largest head of iceberg lettuce you can find and save any leftovers for sandwiches or salads. If you don't have enough large leaves, simply overlap two smaller leaves.

NUTRITIONAL INFORMATION, PER SERVING: about 230 cal, 16 g pro, 13 g total fat (2 g sat. fat), 15 g carb, 3 g fibre, 64 mg chol, 249 mg sodium, 578 mg potassium. % RDI: 10% calcium, 19% iron, 58% vit A, 35% vit C, 39% folate.

A few fresh basil leaves scattered over the finished pasta add a fresh flavour note.

Tomato and Seafood Penne

HANDS-ON TIME	•	TOTAL TIME	•	MAKES
25 MINUTES		25 MINUTES		4 SERVINGS

What you need

225 g	whole wheat penne
2 tsp	olive oil
3	shallots, chopped
2	leeks (white and light green parts only), halved lengthwise and thinly sliced crosswise
3	cloves garlic, minced
2 cups	canned no-salt-added diced tomatoes
1 tsp	dried oregano
pinch	hot pepper flakes
pinch	each salt and pepper
170 g	jumbo sea scallops (about 10), halved
170 g	jumbo shrimp (21 to 24 count), peeled, deveined and halved lengthwise
6 cups	packed baby spinach
⅓ cup	grated Parmesan cheese
¼ cup	chopped fresh basil

How to make it

In large saucepan of boiling water, cook pasta according to package instructions until al dente. Reserving ¼ cup of the cooking liquid, drain pasta.

While pasta is cooking, in large nonstick skillet, heat oil over medium heat; cook shallots, leeks and garlic, stirring occasionally, until softened, about 5 minutes. Stir in tomatoes, oregano, hot pepper flakes, salt and pepper; simmer for 5 minutes.

Stir in scallops and shrimp; cook, stirring occasionally, until shrimp are pink and scallops are opaque throughout, about 3 minutes.

Stir in pasta and spinach; cook until spinach is wilted, about 2 minutes. Stir in enough of the reserved cooking liquid to coat; transfer to serving platter. Sprinkle with Parmesan and basil.

TIP FROM THE TEST KITCHEN
When you make pasta, always reserve some of the cooking liquid before draining. This starchy liquid loosens your sauce and helps it cling to the pasta.

NUTRITIONAL INFORMATION, PER SERVING: about 385 cal, 28 g pro, 7 g total fat (2 g sat. fat), 58 g carb, 8 g fibre, 70 mg chol, 305 mg sodium, 580 mg potassium. % RDI: 27% calcium, 41% iron, 58% vit A, 30% vit C, 44% folate.

Rapini and Shrimp Pasta

HANDS-ON TIME	•	TOTAL TIME	•	MAKES
35 MINUTES		35 MINUTES		4 TO 6 SERVINGS

What you need

3 tbsp	extra-virgin olive oil
1	red finger chili pepper
3	cloves garlic, thinly sliced
5	anchovy fillets, chopped
3 tbsp	capers, drained and rinsed
1⅔ cups	bottled strained tomatoes (passata)
450 g	large shrimp (31 to 40 count), peeled and deveined
pinch	each salt and pepper
1	bunch (340 g) rapini
1	pkg (360 g) fresh lasagna sheets, cut in thick strips (see tip, below)

How to make it

In Dutch oven or large heavy-bottomed saucepan, heat oil over medium-high heat. Prick chili pepper 4 times with fork; add to oil. Add garlic, anchovies and capers; cook, stirring, for 2 minutes. Stir in ¼ cup water, scraping up browned bits from bottom of pan until dissolved.

Add tomatoes and bring to boil; reduce heat and simmer until reduced by half, about 7 minutes.

Sprinkle shrimp with salt and pepper; add to pan and simmer for 3 minutes.

While tomato mixture is simmering, trim ½ inch (1 cm) off base of rapini stems; cut rapini into thirds. In large saucepan of boiling salted water, cook rapini until tender, about 4 minutes. Using slotted spoon, remove rapini and drain; stir into tomato mixture.

Add pasta to same saucepan of boiling salted water; cook according to package instructions until al dente. Drain and add to tomato mixture; toss to coat.

TIP FROM THE TEST KITCHEN
Look for fresh lasagna sheets in the deli section of your supermarket.

NUTRITIONAL INFORMATION, PER EACH OF 6 SERVINGS:
about 332 cal, 21 g pro, 10 g total fat (1 g sat. fat), 39 g carb,
3 g fibre, 133 mg chol, 761 mg sodium, 279 mg potassium. % RDI:
11% calcium, 40% iron, 19% vit A, 23% vit C, 57% folate.

Linguine With Tuna and Mushrooms

HANDS-ON TIME		**TOTAL TIME**		**MAKES**
30 MINUTES	•	40 MINUTES	•	4 TO 6 SERVINGS

What you need

2	large tomatoes (450 g)
2 tbsp	extra-virgin olive oil
1 tbsp	unsalted butter
2	cloves garlic, smashed
225 g	button mushrooms, thinly sliced
pinch	each salt and pepper
2	anchovy fillets, rinsed and drained
340 g	linguine
2	cans (each 80 g) oil-packed tuna, drained
3 tbsp	chopped fresh parsley

How to make it

Score X in bottom of each tomato. In large saucepan of boiling water, cook tomatoes until skins begin to split, 20 to 30 seconds. Using slotted spoon, transfer to bowl of ice water; chill for 1 minute. Peel off and discard skins; seed and dice tomatoes. Set aside.

In large skillet, heat 1 tbsp of the oil and the butter over medium heat; cook 1 of the garlic cloves, stirring, until golden, about 1 minute. Discard garlic. Add mushrooms, salt and pepper; cook, stirring occasionally, until tender and golden, about 6 minutes. Transfer to plate.

In same skillet, heat remaining oil over medium heat; cook remaining garlic, stirring, until golden, about 1 minute. Discard garlic. Add anchovies; cook, stirring, until dissolved, about 20 seconds.

While mushrooms are cooking, in large saucepan of boiling salted water, cook pasta according to package instructions until al dente. Reserving 1 cup of the cooking liquid, drain pasta; return to pan.

Stir tomatoes and ⅓ cup of the reserved cooking liquid into anchovies; simmer, stirring occasionally, until slightly thickened, about 5 minutes.

Stir tuna into tomato mixture; cook for 2 minutes. Stir in parsley and mushrooms; cook for 1 minute. Stir tomato mixture into pasta, adding enough of the remaining reserved cooking liquid to coat; cook for 1 minute.

NUTRITIONAL INFORMATION, PER EACH OF 6 SERVINGS:
about 332 cal, 16 g pro, 10 g total fat (2 g sat. fat), 46 g carb,
4 g fibre, 10 mg chol, 297 mg sodium, 373 mg potassium. % RDI:
2% calcium, 21% iron, 9% vit A, 17% vit C, 59% folate.

Fisherman-Style Bucatini

HANDS-ON TIME	•	TOTAL TIME	•	MAKES
30 MINUTES		30 MINUTES		4 TO 6 SERVINGS

What you need

2 tbsp	extra-virgin olive oil
1	shallot, minced
¼ cup	chopped fresh parsley
¼ tsp	dried sage
¼ tsp	each salt and pepper
450 g	frozen mixed seafood, thawed (see tip, below)
340 g	large shrimp (31 to 40 count), peeled and deveined
⅓ cup	dry white wine
1 cup	bottled strained tomatoes (passata)
340 g	bucatini

How to make it

In large skillet, heat oil over medium heat; cook shallot, 2 tbsp of the parsley, the sage, salt and pepper, stirring, just until shallot is beginning to brown, about 3 minutes.

Stir in seafood and shrimp; cook, stirring, for 2 minutes. Stir in wine; boil until reduced by half, about 3 minutes.

Stir in tomatoes; reduce heat, cover and simmer until shrimp are pink and seafood is opaque throughout, about 5 minutes.

While seafood mixture is cooking, in large saucepan of boiling salted water, cook pasta according to package instructions until al dente. Reserving 1 cup of the cooking liquid, drain pasta; return to pan.

Stir seafood mixture into pasta, adding enough of the reserved cooking liquid to coat; cook for 1 minute. Sprinkle with remaining parsley.

TIP FROM THE TEST KITCHEN

Using frozen mixed seafood in this recipe saves prep time, because every piece is shucked, shelled and trimmed for you. You can substitute your favourite fresh seafood, such as squid, octopus, mussels and clams if you like. Use 450 g, making sure to weigh your seafood after it has been peeled, shelled or shucked.

NUTRITIONAL INFORMATION, PER EACH OF 6 SERVINGS:
about 379 cal, 27 g pro, 7 g total fat (1 g sat. fat), 47 g carb, 3 g fibre, 129 mg chol, 709 mg sodium, 256 mg potassium. % RDI: 8% calcium, 45% iron, 5% vit A, 13% vit C, 57% folate.

Lobster Fettuccine for Two

HANDS-ON TIME	TOTAL TIME	MAKES
15 MINUTES	25 MINUTES	2 SERVINGS

What you need

2	cooked lobsters (900 g total), see tip, below
225 g	fettuccine
1 tbsp	olive oil
2	cloves garlic, minced
1	shallot, minced
½ tsp	salt
pinch	hot pepper flakes
¼ cup	dry white wine
¼ cup	finely chopped fresh parsley
¼ cup	whipping cream (35%)

How to make it

Place 1 lobster on cutting board; twist off tail. Using sharp chef's knife, cut tail in half lengthwise; remove meat from tail and cut into chunks. Place in bowl.

Remove claws from body. With blunt side of knife, crack claws; pull apart shell and remove meat. Cut into chunks and add to bowl. Pull off back shell; remove white protein clumps and discard. Add green or yellow tomalley (liver) to bowl, if desired. Reserve shells for stock, if desired. Repeat with remaining lobster. (*Make-ahead: Cover and refrigerate for up to 2 hours.*)

In large saucepan of boiling salted water, cook pasta according to package instructions until al dente. Reserving ¼ cup of the cooking liquid, drain pasta; return to pan.

While pasta is cooking, in large nonstick skillet, heat oil over medium heat; cook lobster, garlic, shallot, salt and hot pepper flakes, stirring, until fragrant, about 1 minute. Add wine; cook, stirring, for 1 minute.

Stir parsley, cream and pasta into lobster mixture, adding enough of the reserved cooking liquid to coat. Cook for 1 minute.

TIP FROM THE TEST KITCHEN

If you're short on prep time, you can use frozen lobster meat instead of fresh (though it will be less firm). Substitute 1 can (320 g) frozen lobster, thawed, drained and squeezed dry.

NUTRITIONAL INFORMATION, PER SERVING: about 728 cal, 41 g pro, 20 g total fat (8 g sat. fat), 89 g carb, 5 g fibre, 130 mg chol, 1,419 mg sodium. % RDI: 13% calcium, 26% iron, 17% vit A, 15% vit C, 82% folate.

Spaghettini With Clams and Bread Crumbs

HANDS-ON TIME	•	TOTAL TIME	•	MAKES
25 MINUTES		50 MINUTES		4 TO 6 SERVINGS

What you need

2 tbsp	butter
2	cloves garlic, minced
1 cup	fresh bread crumbs
¼ cup	chopped fresh parsley
¼ cup	extra-virgin olive oil
1	onion, chopped
4	anchovy fillets, minced
1 tbsp	capers, drained and chopped
⅓ cup	dry white wine
1	can (142 g) whole baby clams
1	can (796 mL) whole tomatoes, drained
pinch	each salt and pepper
340 g	spaghettini

How to make it

In nonstick skillet, melt butter over medium heat; cook half of the garlic and the bread crumbs, stirring often, until golden, about 5 minutes. Stir in 2 tbsp of the parsley; cook for 1 minute. Transfer to bowl.

In saucepan, heat half of the oil over medium heat; cook onion, stirring, until softened, about 5 minutes. Stir in anchovies, capers and remaining garlic; cook, stirring, until fragrant, about 2 minutes.

Stir in wine, clams, tomatoes, salt and pepper, breaking up tomatoes with spoon. Bring to boil; reduce heat and simmer for 25 minutes.

While clam mixture is simmering, cook pasta according to package instructions until al dente. Drain pasta; stir pasta, and remaining oil and parsley into clam mixture. Scrape onto serving platter; sprinkle with bread crumb mixture.

NUTRITIONAL INFORMATION, PER EACH OF 6 SERVINGS:
about 391 cal, 12 g pro, 15 g total fat (4 g sat. fat), 52 g carb, 4 g fibre, 19 mg chol, 487 mg sodium, 357 mg potassium. % RDI: 7% calcium, 44% iron, 8% vit A, 30% vit C, 62% folate.

Spicy Asian Crab Noodle Salad

HANDS-ON TIME	•	TOTAL TIME	•	MAKES
1 HOUR		1 HOUR		8 SERVINGS

What you need

COCONUT LIME DRESSING:

½ cup	coconut milk
¼ tsp	grated lime zest
3 tbsp	lime juice
4 tsp	vegetable oil
1½ tsp	liquid honey
1 tsp	Asian chili sauce (such as sriracha)
1	small clove garlic, finely grated or pressed
1 tsp	grated fresh ginger
1 tsp	salt
¾ tsp	fish sauce
pinch	pepper

SALAD:

750 g	frozen cooked snow crab clusters, thawed
3 cups	snow peas (about 225 g), trimmed and thinly sliced
half	pkg (450 g pkg) rice stick noodles (⅛ inch/3 mm wide)
½ tsp	vegetable oil
2 cups	matchstick-cut carrots
1	red finger chili pepper, seeded and thinly sliced
1 cup	chopped fresh cilantro
1	avocado, pitted, peeled and diced
2 tbsp	unsalted cashews, toasted and chopped
	lime wedges (optional)

How to make it

COCONUT LIME DRESSING: Whisk together coconut milk, lime zest, lime juice, oil, honey, chili sauce, garlic, ginger, salt, fish sauce and pepper. Set aside. *(Make-ahead: Cover and refrigerate for up to 24 hours.)*

SALAD: Crack snow crab legs; remove meat and transfer to colander, squeezing out excess liquid. Discard shells. Set meat aside.

In large saucepan of boiling water, cook snow peas until tender-crisp, about 30 seconds. Using slotted spoon, transfer to bowl of ice water; chill for 1 minute. Drain. Set aside.

While snow peas are cooking, prepare noodles according to package instructions; drain and rinse under cold water. Drain well; toss with oil to coat.

In large bowl, toss together snow peas, noodles, crab, carrots, chili pepper and ¾ cup of the cilantro. Add Coconut Lime Dressing; toss gently to coat. Top with avocado, cashews and remaining cilantro. Serve with lime wedges (if using).

TIP FROM THE TEST KITCHEN
Rice noodles absorb the dressing quickly, so serve the salad immediately.

NUTRITIONAL INFORMATION, PER SERVING: about 262 cal, 10 g pro, 11 g total fat (4 g sat. fat), 32 g carb, 4 g fibre, 20 mg chol, 566 mg sodium, 371 mg potassium. % RDI: 4% calcium, 16% iron, 36% vit A, 38% vit C, 23% folate.

Garlic Shrimp With Rice Noodles

HANDS-ON TIME	•	TOTAL TIME	•	MAKES
20 MINUTES		20 MINUTES		4 SERVINGS

What you need

400 g	rice stick noodles (¼ inch/5 mm wide)
3 tbsp	vegetable oil
½ cup	sliced shallots
1 tsp	chopped Thai bird's-eye pepper
4	cloves garlic, minced
340 g	large shrimp (31 to 40 count), peeled and deveined
4	baby bok choy, sliced lengthwise
1	can (398 mL) baby corn cobs, drained
1 cup	chicken or vegetable broth
2 tbsp	fish sauce
1 tbsp	cornstarch
1 cup	fresh Thai basil or basil leaves
	lime wedges

How to make it

Prepare noodles according to package instructions. Drain; keep warm.

While noodles are cooking, in wok or large nonstick skillet, heat oil over medium-high heat; cook shallots, stirring, just until beginning to brown, about 3 minutes. Add Thai pepper and garlic; cook, stirring, for 30 seconds.

Add shrimp; cook, stirring, just until beginning to turn pink, about 2 minutes. Add bok choy and corn cobs; cook, stirring, for 1 minute. Stir in broth and fish sauce; cook, stirring occasionally, until vegetables are tender, 1 to 2 minutes.

Whisk cornstarch with 2 tbsp water; stir into shrimp mixture. Return to boil; stir in basil. Serve shrimp mixture over noodles with lime wedges.

NUTRITIONAL INFORMATION, PER SERVING: about 582 cal, 21 g pro, 13 g total fat (1 g sat. fat), 94 g carb, 6 g fibre, 97 mg chol, 1,733 mg sodium. % RDI: 9% calcium, 23% iron, 14% vit A, 37% vit C, 21% folate.

Leave the tail shell on when you peel shrimp. It looks nice, and the shell adds a little extra flavour to the dish.

Pea Shoot and Shrimp Risotto

HANDS-ON TIME	•	**TOTAL TIME**	•	**MAKES**
55 MINUTES		55 MINUTES		4 SERVINGS

What you need

450 g	super colossal shrimp (8 to 12 count), peeled and deveined (tail-on)
3 tbsp	extra-virgin olive oil
1 tbsp	lemon juice
1	clove garlic, minced
½ tsp	salt
¼ tsp	pepper
1½ cups	sodium-reduced chicken broth
1	leek (white and light green parts only), finely diced
1 cup	arborio rice
¼ cup	dry white wine
115 g	pea shoots or pea sprouts, coarsely chopped
⅓ cup	shaved Parmesan cheese

How to make it

In bowl, toss shrimp with 1 tbsp of the oil, the lemon juice, garlic, ¼ tsp of the salt and the pepper; let stand for 10 minutes. Place on greased grill over medium-high heat; close lid and grill, turning once, until shrimp are pink and opaque throughout, 6 to 8 minutes. Keep warm.

While shrimp are marinating, in small saucepan, bring broth and 1½ cups water to boil; reduce heat to low and keep warm.

In large saucepan, heat remaining oil over medium heat; cook leek and remaining salt, stirring occasionally, until softened, about 4 minutes. Add rice, stirring to coat and toast grains. Add wine; cook, stirring, until no liquid remains, about 2 minutes.

Add ½ cup of the broth mixture; cook, stirring, until most of the liquid is absorbed. Continue adding 2 cups of the remaining broth mixture, ½ cup at a time and stirring after each addition until most of the liquid is absorbed before adding more, about 20 minutes total. (Rice should be loose, creamy but not mushy and still slightly firm in centre of kernel.)

Stir in pea shoots and remaining broth; cook until pea shoots are slightly wilted, about 3 minutes. Top with shrimp; sprinkle with Parmesan.

TIP FROM THE TEST KITCHEN
You can broil the shrimp instead of grilling it, if you like.

NUTRITIONAL INFORMATION, PER SERVING: about 412 cal, 25 g pro, 14 g total fat (3 g sat. fat), 44 g carb, 2 g fibre, 134 mg chol, 753 mg sodium, 246 mg potassium. % RDI: 13% calcium, 21% iron, 15% vit A, 28% vit C, 14% folate.

Quick Salmon Kedgeree

HANDS-ON TIME	TOTAL TIME	MAKES
20 MINUTES	35 MINUTES	4 SERVINGS

What you need

340 g	skinless salmon fillet
1 tbsp	curry powder
¼ tsp	each salt and pepper
2 tsp	canola oil
1	small onion, finely chopped
2	cloves garlic, minced
2 cups	sodium-reduced chicken broth
1 cup	20-minute whole grain brown rice (see tip, below)
3 cups	shredded stemmed kale
½ cup	frozen peas
2	eggs, lightly beaten
1 cup	grape or cherry tomatoes, halved
1 tbsp	lemon juice

How to make it

Sprinkle both sides of fish with a pinch each of the curry powder, salt and pepper. Set aside.

In small saucepan, heat 1½ tsp of the oil over medium-high heat; cook onion, garlic, and remaining curry powder, salt and pepper, stirring, until onion is softened, about 3 minutes. Stir in broth and rice; bring to boil. Reduce heat, cover and simmer until almost no liquid remains, about 15 minutes.

Stir in kale and peas; cover and cook until no liquid remains and rice is tender, about 5 minutes. Remove from heat; let stand, covered, for 5 minutes. Fluff with fork.

While rice is cooking, in small nonstick skillet, heat remaining oil over medium heat; cook eggs, stirring, just until set, about 2 minutes. Transfer to plate; set aside.

Wipe out skillet; cook fish over medium heat, turning once, until golden on both sides and fish flakes easily when tested, about 7 minutes. Let cool slightly; using fork, break into chunks.

Gently stir tomatoes, salmon, eggs and lemon juice into rice mixture.

TIP FROM THE TEST KITCHEN
Twenty-minute whole grain brown rice is a great option for healthful weeknight meals. It has been parboiled so it cooks much more quickly than raw brown rice.

NUTRITIONAL INFORMATION, PER SERVING: about 446 cal, 28 g pro, 15 g total fat (3 g sat. fat), 52 g carb, 5 g fibre, 133 mg chol, 565 mg sodium, 784 mg potassium. % RDI: 11% calcium, 20% iron, 82% vit A, 103% vit C, 30% folate.

Saffron Brown Rice With Shrimp and Chorizo

HANDS-ON TIME
15 MINUTES

•

TOTAL TIME
35 MINUTES

•

MAKES
4 SERVINGS

What you need

2 tsp	vegetable oil
1	onion, chopped
1 cup	20-minute whole grain brown rice (see tip, opposite)
¼ tsp	saffron threads
2 cups	sodium-reduced chicken broth
¾ cup	sliced dry-cured chorizo
450 g	jumbo shrimp (21 to 24 count), peeled and deveined
3	cloves garlic, minced
pinch	each salt and pepper
1 cup	frozen peas
⅓ cup	fresh cilantro leaves, chopped

How to make it

In large saucepan, heat oil over medium heat; cook onion, stirring often, until tender, about 5 minutes.

Stir in rice and saffron. Add broth and bring to boil; reduce heat, cover and simmer until rice is tender and no liquid remains, about 20 minutes. Let stand, covered, for 10 minutes; fluff with fork.

While rice is cooking, in skillet, cook chorizo over medium heat, stirring occasionally, until lightly browned, about 5 minutes. Stir in shrimp, garlic, salt and pepper; cook, stirring, until garlic is fragrant, about 2 minutes.

Stir in peas; cook, stirring occasionally, until shrimp are pink and opaque throughout, about 2 minutes. Stir in rice mixture; sprinkle with cilantro.

NUTRITIONAL INFORMATION, PER SERVING: about 532 cal, 35 g pro, 21 g total fat (7 g sat. fat), 49 g carb, 4 g fibre, 166 mg chol, 983 mg sodium, 611 mg potassium. % RDI: 8% calcium, 29% iron, 12% vit A, 12% vit C, 16% folate.

Unilateral Salmon Fillets

HANDS-ON TIME	•	TOTAL TIME	•	MAKES
25 MINUTES		25 MINUTES		4 SERVINGS

What you need

4	skin-on salmon fillets (each about 150 g)
¼ tsp	each salt and pepper
3 tbsp	olive oil
½ cup	pine nuts
1	pkg (142 g) baby arugula
½ cup	oil-packed sun-dried tomatoes, drained and thinly sliced
2 tbsp	balsamic vinegar

How to make it

Sprinkle fish with salt and pepper. In large ovenproof skillet, heat 1 tbsp of the oil over medium heat; cook fish, skin side down and without turning, until skin is crisp, 10 to 12 minutes. Transfer skillet to 400°F (200°C) oven; roast until fish flakes easily when tested, 6 to 8 minutes.

While fish is roasting, in small skillet, toast pine nuts over medium heat, stirring occasionally, until golden, 3 to 5 minutes. Coarsely chop. Return pine nuts to skillet; add remaining oil. Cook, stirring, until oil is warmed through, about 1 minute. Keep warm.

Divide arugula among serving plates; top with fish. Sprinkle with sun-dried tomatoes; spoon pine nut mixture over top. Drizzle with vinegar.

TIP FROM THE TEST KITCHEN

Cooking this fish unilaterally, or on one side only, yields crispy skin and tender flesh.

NUTRITIONAL INFORMATION, PER SERVING: about 432 cal, 27 g pro, 33 g total fat (5 g sat. fat), 8 g carb, 2 g fibre, 65 mg chol, 255 mg sodium, 855 mg potassium. % RDI: 8% calcium, 16% iron, 12% vit A, 38% vit C, 36% folate.

Fish Fillets
With Creamy Chanterelle Sauce

HANDS-ON TIME	•	TOTAL TIME	•	MAKES
20 MINUTES		20 MINUTES		4 SERVINGS

What you need

FISH:

750 g	skin-on firm white fish fillets, cut in 4 portions
¼ tsp	salt
1 tbsp	olive oil

CREAMY CHANTERELLE SAUCE:

60 g	pancetta, diced
1	shallot, finely chopped
1 cup	small chanterelle or stemmed shiitake mushrooms
½ cup	dry white wine
½ cup	whipping cream (35%)
1 tsp	lemon juice
1 tbsp	chopped fresh chives

How to make it

FISH: Sprinkle fish with salt. In large skillet, heat oil over medium heat; cook fish, skin side down and turning halfway through, until opaque throughout and fish flakes easily when tested, 8 to 10 minutes. Transfer to serving platter; keep warm.

CREAMY CHANTERELLE SAUCE: While fish is cooking, in separate skillet, cook pancetta over medium heat, stirring often, until crisp, 3 to 5 minutes. Add shallot; cook, stirring, until softened, about 2 minutes. Add chanterelles; cook, stirring occasionally, until softened, about 2 minutes.

Stir in wine; cook, stirring, until reduced by half, about 3 minutes. Stir in cream; bring to boil. Reduce heat and simmer, stirring occasionally, until slightly thickened, about 3 minutes. Stir in lemon juice. Spoon over fish; sprinkle with chives.

TIP FROM THE TEST KITCHEN
Chanterelle stems are nice and tender, so there's no need to remove them. Simply rub the mushrooms clean with a damp paper towel before using.

NUTRITIONAL INFORMATION, PER SERVING: about 381 cal, 39 g pro, 21 g total fat (9 g sat. fat), 3 g carb, 1 g fibre, 106 mg chol, 444 mg sodium, 884 mg potassium. % RDI: 10% calcium, 12% iron, 18% vit A, 2% vit C, 10% folate.

These juicy patties
are also delicious with
a side of tartar sauce.

White Fish Cakes
With Lemon-Chili Mayo

HANDS-ON TIME	•	TOTAL TIME	•	MAKES
20 MINUTES		20 MINUTES		4 SERVINGS

What you need

WHITE FISH CAKES:

1	rib celery, coarsely chopped
2	green onions, coarsely chopped
¼ cup	fresh parsley leaves
450 g	skinless firm white fish fillets (such as halibut), coarsely chopped
¾ cup	fresh bread crumbs (see tip, below)
1	egg
2 tsp	Dijon mustard
¼ tsp	pepper
1 tbsp	vegetable oil

LEMON-CHILI MAYO:

⅓ cup	light mayonnaise
1½ tsp	lemon juice
¼ tsp	chili powder

How to make it

WHITE FISH CAKES: In food processor, pulse together celery, green onions and parsley until finely chopped. Scrape into bowl.

Add fish to food processor; pulse until finely chopped but not puréed. Add to bowl; stir in bread crumbs, egg, mustard and pepper. Divide into 8 portions; form into ½-inch (1 cm) thick patties.

In large nonstick skillet, heat oil over medium heat; working in batches, cook fish cakes, turning once, until golden and firm to the touch, 8 to 10 minutes.

LEMON-CHILI MAYO: While fish cakes are cooking, whisk together mayonnaise, lemon juice and chili powder. Serve with White Fish Cakes.

VARIATION

Cornmeal-Crusted White Fish Cakes With Lemon-Chili Mayo
Dredge fish cakes in ⅓ cup medium- or fine-ground cornmeal. Cook as directed.

TIP FROM THE TEST KITCHEN
To make fresh bread crumbs, tear fresh bread into chunks and pulse it in your food processor until it's in coarse crumbs. To make the ¾ cup for this recipe, you'll need about 1 slice of bread.

NUTRITIONAL INFORMATION, PER SERVING: about 268 cal, 26 g pro, 14 g total fat (2 g sat. fat), 7 g carb, 1 g fibre, 89 mg chol, 300 mg sodium, 619 mg potassium. % RDI: 8% calcium, 14% iron, 13% vit A, 10% vit C, 17% folate.

Potato and Salmon Cakes
With Lemony Mustard Yogurt Sauce

HANDS-ON TIME	TOTAL TIME	MAKES
35 MINUTES	1 HOUR	6 SERVINGS

What you need

LEMONY MUSTARD YOGURT SAUCE:

⅓ cup	2% plain Greek yogurt
¼ cup	light mayonnaise
2 tsp	chopped fresh chives
2 tsp	grainy mustard
2 tsp	lemon juice
pinch	each salt and pepper

POTATO AND SALMON CAKES:

1	skinless salmon fillet (about 170 g)
pinch	salt
1	egg, lightly beaten
2	cloves garlic, minced
2	green onions, thinly sliced
½ cup	dried bread crumbs
2 tbsp	chopped fresh chives
1 tbsp	capers, drained, rinsed and chopped
1 tbsp	grainy mustard
2 tsp	lemon juice
pinch	pepper
2 cups	mashed potatoes (see tip, below)
1 tbsp	olive oil
	lemon wedges

How to make it

LEMONY MUSTARD YOGURT SAUCE: Whisk together yogurt, mayonnaise, chives, mustard, lemon juice, salt and pepper. Cover and refrigerate until ready to use.

POTATO AND SALMON CAKES: Place fish on parchment paper–lined rimmed baking sheet; sprinkle with salt. Bake in 350°F (180°C) oven until fish flakes easily when tested, 12 to 15 minutes. Using fork, break into bite-size pieces.

In large bowl, stir together egg, garlic, green onions, bread crumbs, chives, capers, mustard, lemon juice and pepper. Stir in mashed potatoes until well combined; gently fold in fish. Shape into twelve ½-inch (1 cm) thick patties; refrigerate for 15 minutes.

In large nonstick skillet, heat oil over medium heat; working in batches, cook patties, turning once, until golden and crispy outside and hot in centre, 8 to 10 minutes. Serve with lemon wedges and Lemony Mustard Yogurt Sauce.

TIP FROM THE TEST KITCHEN
Taste the mashed potatoes before adding them to the fish mixture. If the potatoes aren't well-seasoned, add an extra pinch of salt.

NUTRITIONAL INFORMATION, PER SERVING: about 200 cal, 10 g pro, 12 g total fat (2 g sat. fat), 15 g carb, 2 g fibre, 49 mg chol, 368 mg sodium, 265 mg potassium. % RDI: 5% calcium, 7% iron, 4% vit A, 8% vit C, 13% folate.

Cracker Catfish With Swiss Chard

HANDS-ON TIME	•	TOTAL TIME	•	MAKES
25 MINUTES		45 MINUTES		4 SERVINGS

What you need

CRACKER CATFISH:

2	skinless catfish fillets (each about 250 g)
½ cup	buttermilk
1 tbsp	Dijon mustard
¾ cup	crushed salted soda crackers (about 20)
2 tbsp	chopped fresh parsley
1 tsp	sweet paprika
½ tsp	each garlic powder and salt
3 tbsp	vegetable oil

SWISS CHARD:

2 tbsp	extra-virgin olive oil
1	clove garlic, thinly sliced
¼ tsp	each salt and hot pepper flakes
1	bunch Swiss chard, coarsely chopped (about 6 cups)
	lemon wedges

How to make it

CRACKER CATFISH: Cut fish diagonally in half; place in glass bowl. Whisk buttermilk with mustard; pour over fish, turning to coat. Refrigerate for 10 minutes.

In shallow dish, combine crackers, parsley, paprika, garlic powder and salt. Dip fish into crumb mixture, turning to coat. Transfer to waxed paper–lined rimmed baking sheet. Cover and refrigerate for 10 minutes or for up to 1 hour.

In large skillet, heat oil over medium-high heat; working in batches, fry fish, turning once, until golden and fish flakes easily when tested, 8 to 10 minutes per batch.

SWISS CHARD: While fish is cooking, in separate skillet, heat oil over medium-high heat; cook garlic, salt and hot pepper flakes, stirring, for 1 minute. Add Swiss chard; cook, stirring, until tender, about 5 minutes. Serve with Cracker Catfish and lemon wedges.

NUTRITIONAL INFORMATION, PER SERVING: about 411 cal, 25 g pro, 25 g total fat (5 g sat. fat), 24 g carb, 6 g fibre, 61 mg chol, 1,199 mg sodium, 1,756 mg potassium. % RDI: 19% calcium, 50% iron, 82% vit A, 78% vit C, 18% folate.

Trout Meunière

HANDS-ON TIME	TOTAL TIME	MAKES
15 MINUTES	15 MINUTES	4 SERVINGS

What you need

¼ cup	all-purpose flour
½ tsp	each salt and pepper
4	skin-on trout fillets (each 170 g)
¼ cup	unsalted butter
2 tbsp	chopped fresh parsley
2 tbsp	lemon juice

How to make it

In shallow dish, whisk together flour, salt and pepper. Dredge fish in flour mixture, shaking off excess.

In large skillet, melt half of the butter over medium heat; cook fish, turning once, until golden and fish flakes easily when tested, 6 to 8 minutes. Transfer to serving plates; keep warm.

Add remaining butter to skillet; cook until butter stops foaming, about 1 minute. Whisk in parsley and lemon juice. Pour over fish.

TIP FROM THE TEST KITCHEN
Serve this trout with boiled or mashed potatoes to soak up all the delicious buttery sauce.

NUTRITIONAL INFORMATION, PER SERVING: about 351 cal, 36 g pro, 21 g total fat (10 g sat. fat), 3 g carb, trace fibre, 131 mg chol, 179 mg sodium, 795 mg potassium. % RDI: 11% calcium, 6% iron, 25% vit A, 17% vit C, 13% folate.

Patting scallops dry before searing guarantees a golden, crisp crust.

Curry-Seared Scallops With Creamy Leeks

HANDS-ON TIME	**TOTAL TIME**	**MAKES**
20 MINUTES	25 MINUTES	4 SERVINGS

What you need

2 tbsp	butter
4	leeks (white and light green parts only), chopped
½ tsp	pepper
½ tsp	salt
½ cup	whipping cream (35%)
pinch	nutmeg
12	jumbo sea scallops (675 g)
½ tsp	curry powder
1 tbsp	olive oil

How to make it

In saucepan, melt butter over medium-high heat; add leeks, pepper, all but a pinch of the salt and ⅓ cup water. Cook, stirring occasionally, until tender, about 10 minutes. Reduce heat to low; stir in cream and nutmeg. Cover and cook until thickened, about 5 minutes.

While sauce is cooking, pat scallops dry; sprinkle with curry powder and remaining salt. In skillet, heat oil over medium-high heat; cook scallops, turning once, until golden brown outside and opaque throughout, about 5 minutes. Serve over leek mixture.

VARIATION

Curry-Seared Shrimp With Creamy Leeks

Substitute 12 colossal shrimp (12 to 15 count) for the scallops.

TIP FROM THE TEST KITCHEN

A tough little muscle runs up the side of a scallop and serves as a "foot" to anchor the mollusk in place. If it's still attached, remove it before cooking. Look for a darker or pinkish area along the edge and peel it off with your fingers.

NUTRITIONAL INFORMATION, PER SERVING: about 314 cal, 22 g pro, 21 g total fat (11 g sat. fat), 10 g carb, 1 g fibre, 100 mg chol, 583 mg sodium, 554 mg potassium. % RDI: 15% calcium, 29% iron, 18% vit A, 8% vit C, 19% folate.

Pan-Fried Tilapia
With Olive Salsa and Spinach Orzo

HANDS-ON TIME		TOTAL TIME		MAKES
25 MINUTES	•	25 MINUTES	•	4 SERVINGS

What you need

OLIVE SALSA:

¼ cup	cherry tomatoes, diced
2 tbsp	finely chopped Kalamata olives
1 tbsp	finely chopped fresh parsley
1 tsp	olive oil

SPINACH ORZO:

1 cup	orzo
2 tsp	olive oil
3	cloves garlic, minced
8 cups	baby spinach
1 cup	cherry tomatoes, quartered
2 tbsp	chopped fresh dill
2 tbsp	lemon juice
¼ tsp	each salt and pepper

PAN-FRIED TILAPIA:

1 tbsp	butter
2	skinless tilapia fillets (each about 225 g), halved lengthwise
pinch	each salt and pepper

How to make it

OLIVE SALSA: Stir together tomatoes, olives, parsley and oil. Set aside.

SPINACH ORZO: In saucepan of boiling salted water, cook orzo according to package instructions until al dente. Drain; set aside.

In nonstick skillet, heat oil over medium heat; cook garlic, stirring, until softened, about 1 minute. Add spinach; cook, stirring, until wilted, about 3 minutes. Stir into orzo. Stir in tomatoes, dill, lemon juice, salt and pepper. Set aside.

PAN-FRIED TILAPIA: While orzo is cooking, in nonstick skillet, melt butter over medium heat. Sprinkle fish with salt and pepper; cook, turning once, until fish flakes easily when tested, about 6 minutes.

TO FINISH: Arrange fish on plates; top with Olive Salsa. Serve with Spinach Orzo.

NUTRITIONAL INFORMATION, PER SERVING: about 355 cal, 31 g pro, 10 g total fat (3 g sat. fat), 37 g carb, 4 g fibre, 64 mg chol, 341 mg sodium, 781 mg potassium. % RDI: 10% calcium, 25% iron, 68% vit A, 27% vit C, 56% folate.

Use any leftover Olive Salsa to top pan-fried chicken or spread on crusty bread as an appetizer on another night.

Blackened Arctic Char With Asparagus Orzo

HANDS-ON TIME	TOTAL TIME	MAKES
20 MINUTES	20 MINUTES	4 SERVINGS

What you need

BLACKENED ARCTIC CHAR:

2 tbsp	sweet paprika
2 tsp	each dried thyme and dried oregano
1½ tsp	chili powder
pinch	cayenne pepper
4	skin-on arctic char fillets (each about 115 g), see tip, below
¼ tsp	each salt and pepper
1 tbsp	olive oil

ASPARAGUS ORZO:

1 cup	orzo
1	bunch (450 g) asparagus, trimmed and cut in 1½-inch (4 cm) pieces
2 tbsp	grated Parmesan cheese
¼ tsp	grated lemon zest
1 tbsp	lemon juice
2 tsp	unsalted butter
¼ tsp	each salt and pepper
2 tbsp	torn fresh basil leaves

How to make it

BLACKENED ARCTIC CHAR: In shallow dish, stir together paprika, thyme, oregano, chili powder and cayenne pepper. Sprinkle fish with salt and pepper; dredge in paprika mixture, turning to coat both sides and shaking off excess.

In large nonstick skillet, heat oil over medium-high heat; cook fish, turning once, until dark golden, about 4 minutes. Reduce heat to medium; cook, turning once, until fish flakes easily when tested, 3 to 5 minutes.

ASPARAGUS ORZO: While fish is cooking, in large saucepan of boiling lightly salted water, cook orzo for 2 minutes less than package instructions for al dente. Add asparagus; cook until orzo is al dente and asparagus is tender-crisp, about 2 minutes. Reserving ¼ cup of the cooking liquid, drain orzo mixture. Return to pan.

Stir in Parmesan, lemon zest, lemon juice, butter, salt and pepper, adding enough of the reserved cooking liquid to lightly coat. Stir in half of the basil. Serve with Blackened Arctic Char; sprinkle with remaining basil.

TIP FROM THE TEST KITCHEN
You can use salmon instead of arctic char, but choose fish raised in recirculating aquaculture systems. Most farmed salmon comes from open-net pens, which are not considered eco-friendly.

NUTRITIONAL INFORMATION, PER SERVING: about 379 cal, 32 g pro, 11 g total fat (3 g sat. fat), 40 g carb, 5 g fibre, 74 mg chol, 809 mg sodium, 750 mg potassium. % RDI: 10% calcium, 29% iron, 34% vit A, 25% vit C, 79% folate.

Arctic char looks like salmon but has a milder flavour. If you can't find it, use rainbow trout or sustainably raised salmon instead.

Crispy Salmon on Braised Vegetables and Spinach Mash

HANDS-ON TIME	TOTAL TIME	MAKES
15 MINUTES	45 MINUTES	4 SERVINGS

What you need

SPINACH MASH:

4	russet potatoes (about 790 g), peeled and cut in chunks
½ cup	warm milk
2 tbsp	butter
1 tbsp	chopped fresh tarragon
2 tsp	prepared horseradish
½ tsp	salt
¼ tsp	pepper
3 cups	packed trimmed fresh spinach, thickly sliced

BRAISED VEGETABLES:

1 tbsp	extra-virgin olive oil
6	cloves garlic, thinly sliced
3 cups	cherry or grape tomatoes
4 tsp	chopped fresh thyme
2 tsp	liquid honey
¾ tsp	pepper
½ tsp	salt
1½ cups	fresh or frozen corn kernels
1	zucchini, diced
4 tsp	butter

CRISPY SALMON:

4	skin-on salmon fillets (each about 170 g), patted dry
pinch	each salt and pepper
4 tsp	olive oil

How to make it

SPINACH MASH: In large saucepan of boiling salted water, cook potatoes until tender, 18 to 20 minutes. Drain well. Mash in milk, butter, tarragon, horseradish, salt and pepper until smooth. Stir in spinach; keep warm.

BRAISED VEGETABLES: While potatoes are cooking, in large skillet, heat oil over medium heat; cook garlic, stirring often, until slightly softened and fragrant, about 1 minute. Add tomatoes, thyme, honey, pepper, salt and ½ cup water; cook, stirring occasionally and mashing gently, until sauce is thickened, about 12 minutes.

Add corn and zucchini, stirring to coat and adding 2 tbsp water if mixture appears dry; cook, stirring occasionally, until vegetables are tender-crisp, about 5 minutes. Stir in butter until melted.

CRISPY SALMON: While tomato mixture is cooking, sprinkle flesh side of fish with salt and pepper. In large nonstick skillet, heat oil over medium heat; cook fish, skin side down and without turning, until skin is crisp and releases easily from pan, about 10 minutes. Turn and cook until fish flakes easily when tested, 1 to 2 minutes.

TO FINISH: Spoon Spinach Mash into centre of serving bowls; surround with Braised Vegetables. Place Crispy Salmon, skin side up, over top.

TIP FROM THE TEST KITCHEN

Don't turn the salmon too early. If it's sticking to the pan, it's not ready to be flipped.

NUTRITIONAL INFORMATION, PER SERVING: about 686 cal, 37 g pro, 36 g total fat (11 g sat. fat), 58 g carb, 7 g fibre, 111 mg chol, 1,072 mg sodium, 1,710 mg potassium. % RDI: 12% calcium, 21% iron, 50% vit A, 67% vit C, 62% folate.

Seared Salmon
With Buttery Couscous and Mango Salsa

HANDS-ON TIME	**TOTAL TIME**	**MAKES**
15 MINUTES	15 MINUTES	4 SERVINGS

What you need

BUTTERY COUSCOUS:

1 cup	Israeli couscous (see tip, below)
3	green onions, sliced
¼ cup	chopped fresh chives
4 tsp	butter
pinch	each salt and pepper

SEARED SALMON:

4	skinless salmon fillets (each about 115 g)
¼ tsp	each salt and pepper
1 tsp	olive oil

MANGO SALSA:

1 cup	diced pitted peeled mango
⅓ cup	diced red onion
3 tbsp	chopped fresh cilantro
½ tsp	grated lime zest
1 tbsp	lime juice
pinch	each salt, pepper and cayenne pepper

How to make it

BUTTERY COUSCOUS: In saucepan, cook couscous according to package instructions. In large bowl, combine green onions, chives, butter, salt and pepper; stir in couscous until butter is melted. Keep warm.

SEARED SALMON: While couscous is cooking, sprinkle fish with salt and pepper. In nonstick skillet, heat oil over medium heat; cook fish, turning once, until fish flakes easily when tested, about 8 minutes.

MANGO SALSA: While fish is cooking, stir together mango, red onion, cilantro, lime zest, lime juice, salt, pepper and cayenne pepper.

TO FINISH: Spoon Buttery Couscous onto serving plates; top with Seared Salmon and Mango Salsa.

TIP FROM THE TEST KITCHEN

Israeli couscous is also called pearl couscous. Look for it in the pasta section or the international aisle of your supermarket.

NUTRITIONAL INFORMATION, PER SERVING: about 399 cal, 25 g pro, 16 g total fat (5 g sat. fat), 37 g carb, 2 g fibre, 67 mg chol, 379 mg sodium, 544 mg potassium. % RDI: 4% calcium, 9% iron, 10% vit A, 32% vit C, 30% folate.

Shrimp With Edamame Succotash

HANDS-ON TIME	**TOTAL TIME**	**MAKES**
25 MINUTES	30 MINUTES	4 SERVINGS

What you need

3	strips sodium-reduced bacon, chopped
450 g	extra-jumbo shrimp (16 to 20 count), peeled and deveined
¼ tsp	pepper
2 tsp	olive oil
1	small onion, diced
half	sweet red pepper, diced
3	cloves garlic, chopped
3 cups	frozen corn kernels
1½ cups	frozen shelled edamame
pinch	salt
3 tbsp	herb-and-garlic cream cheese
1 tbsp	lemon juice
¼ cup	chopped fresh cilantro

How to make it

In nonstick skillet, cook bacon over medium heat, stirring occasionally, until crisp, 4 to 6 minutes. Using slotted spoon, transfer to paper towel–lined plate; let drain.

Drain all but 1 tsp fat from skillet. Add shrimp to skillet; cook, stirring occasionally, until pink and opaque throughout, 3 to 4 minutes. Sprinkle with a pinch of the pepper; transfer to plate and keep warm.

In same skillet, heat oil over medium heat; cook onion, red pepper and garlic, stirring, until softened, 3 to 4 minutes. Add corn, edamame, salt and remaining pepper; cook, stirring, until heated through, about 6 minutes.

Stir in cream cheese until melted. Stir in bacon and lemon juice. Serve shrimp over corn mixture; sprinkle with cilantro.

VARIATION

Scallops With Edamame Succotash
Replace shrimp with 12 jumbo sea scallops; cook, turning once, until golden outside and opaque throughout, about 4 minutes.

NUTRITIONAL INFORMATION, PER SERVING: about 342 cal, 29 g pro, 12 g total fat (4 g sat. fat), 33 g carb, 5 g fibre, 149 mg chol, 236 mg sodium, 776 mg potassium. % RDI: 9% calcium, 28% iron, 15% vit A, 58% vit C, 90% folate.

Lime-Marinated Fish With Chili Sambal

HANDS-ON TIME
45 MINUTES

TOTAL TIME
1¼ HOURS

MAKES
6 TO 8 SERVINGS

What you need

LIME-MARINATED FISH:

900 g	skin-on firm white fish fillets, cut in 8 portions
½ tsp	salt
2 tbsp	lime or lemon juice
½ tsp	pepper
½ cup	peanut oil or vegetable oil

CHILI SAMBAL:

½ cup	chopped shallots
6	red finger chili peppers, seeded and chopped
2	cloves garlic, smashed
1	tomato, peeled, seeded and chopped
2 tsp	chili powder (or ½ tsp cayenne pepper)
2 tsp	finely chopped fresh ginger
1½ tsp	packed brown sugar
¼ tsp	salt
2 tsp	lime or lemon juice

How to make it

LIME-MARINATED FISH: Rub fish all over with salt; drizzle with lime juice. Cover and refrigerate for 30 minutes.

Pat fish dry with paper towel; sprinkle with pepper.

In wok or large nonstick skillet, heat oil over medium-high heat; cook fish, turning once and reducing heat as browning begins, until fish is crispy and flakes easily when tested, about 10 minutes per each 1 inch (2.5 cm) of thickness.

Using slotted spoon, transfer fish to paper towel–lined plate; let drain. Drain all but 2 tbsp oil from wok; set wok aside for Chili Sambal. Transfer fish to serving platter; keep warm.

CHILI SAMBAL: While fish is cooking, in food processor, purée together shallots, chili peppers, garlic, tomato, chili powder, ginger, brown sugar and salt until pasty and almost smooth; set aside.

Heat reserved oil in wok over medium heat; cook shallot mixture, stirring constantly and adding water, 1 tbsp at a time, every few minutes as paste dries, until fragrant, darkened and oil begins to separate, 18 to 20 minutes. Stir in lime juice. Spread over Lime-Marinated Fish.

NUTRITIONAL INFORMATION, PER EACH OF 8 SERVINGS:
about 222 cal, 22 g pro, 12 g total fat (2 g sat. fat), 7 g carb, 1 g fibre, 91 mg chol, 306 mg sodium, 489 mg potassium. % RDI: 3% calcium, 12% iron, 10% vit A, 74% vit C, 10% folate.

Saltwater fish, such as striped bass, is particularly good with this spicy chili paste.

Coconut Shrimp
With Sweet Potato Fries

HANDS-ON TIME	•	TOTAL TIME	•	MAKES
30 MINUTES		30 MINUTES		4 SERVINGS

What you need

SWEET POTATO FRIES:

2	large sweet potatoes (about 750 g), peeled and cut in scant ½-inch (1 cm) thick sticks
2 tsp	olive oil
1 tsp	garlic powder
¼ tsp	each salt and pepper

COCONUT SHRIMP:

2	egg whites, whisked
¼ tsp	pepper
pinch	salt
½ cup	panko bread crumbs
¼ cup	unsweetened desiccated coconut
3 tbsp	all-purpose flour
450 g	jumbo shrimp (21 to 24 count), peeled (tail-on), deveined and patted dry
4 tsp	vegetable oil
⅓ cup	mango chutney (see tip, below)

How to make it

SWEET POTATO FRIES: Toss together sweet potatoes, oil, garlic powder, salt and pepper. Arrange in single layer on parchment paper–lined rimmed baking sheet. Bake in 425°F (220°C) oven, turning once, until tender and light golden, about 25 minutes.

COCONUT SHRIMP: While fries are baking, in shallow bowl, whisk together egg whites, pepper and salt. In separate shallow bowl, stir together panko, coconut and flour. Holding by tail, dip 1 shrimp into egg mixture, shaking off excess. Dip into panko mixture, turning to coat and pressing to adhere. Repeat with remaining shrimp, egg mixture and panko mixture.

In large nonstick skillet, heat 2 tsp of the oil over medium heat; cook half of the shrimp, turning once, until golden, about 6 minutes. Repeat with remaining oil and shrimp. Serve with Sweet Potato Fries and mango chutney.

TIP FROM THE TEST KITCHEN
If you don't have mango chutney, plum sauce makes a delicious dip, too.

NUTRITIONAL INFORMATION, PER SERVING: about 339 cal, 21 g pro, 6 g total fat (3 g sat. fat), 50 g carb, 5 g fibre, 128 mg chol, 607 mg sodium, 586 mg potassium. % RDI: 8% calcium, 26% iron, 261% vit A, 38% vit C, 10% folate.

Seared Scallops
With Bacony Brussels Sprouts

HANDS-ON TIME	•	TOTAL TIME	•	MAKES
20 MINUTES		20 MINUTES		4 SERVINGS

What you need

450 g	brussels sprouts, trimmed
3	strips bacon, chopped
3	cloves garlic, chopped
¼ tsp	each salt and pepper
2 tsp	grated lemon zest
1 tbsp	lemon juice
8	jumbo sea scallops (about 400 g)
1 tbsp	vegetable oil

How to make it

Pull leaves from brussels sprouts and reserve; cut cores in half. Set leaves and cores aside.

In skillet, cook bacon over medium-high heat, stirring, until golden and crisp, about 2 minutes. Using slotted spoon, transfer to paper towel–lined plate; let drain.

Drain all but 2 tsp fat from skillet; cook brussels sprout leaves and cores, and garlic over medium-high heat, stirring occasionally, until cores are beginning to brown, about 5 minutes.

Add half each of the salt and pepper, and ¼ cup water; cook, stirring, until almost no liquid remains, about 4 minutes. Stir in lemon zest and juice. Scrape onto serving platter; top with bacon. Keep warm.

Sprinkle scallops with remaining salt and pepper. In same skillet, heat oil over medium-high heat; cook scallops, turning once, until golden brown and opaque throughout, about 5 minutes. Serve over brussels sprouts mixture.

NUTRITIONAL INFORMATION, PER SERVING: about 208 cal, 22 g pro, 9 g total fat (2 g sat. fat), 12 g carb, 4 g fibre, 40 mg chol, 337 mg sodium, 725 mg potassium. % RDI: 6% calcium, 13% iron, 10% vit A, 127% vit C, 35% folate.

Shrimp, Snow Pea and Carrot Sauté With Brown Butter

HANDS-ON TIME	TOTAL TIME	MAKES
15 MINUTES	15 MINUTES	4 SERVINGS

What you need

2 tbsp	butter
450 g	extra-jumbo shrimp (16 to 20 count), peeled and deveined
2	shallots, halved lengthwise and thinly sliced
6	cloves garlic, minced
1	bunch carrots, halved lengthwise and sliced diagonally in long, thin strips
3 cups	snow peas, trimmed
¼ tsp	each salt and pepper
	lemon wedges

How to make it

In large skillet, melt 2 tsp of the butter over medium-high heat; cook shrimp, stirring, until pink and opaque throughout, about 2 minutes. Transfer to plate.

Add remaining butter to skillet; cook over medium-high heat, stirring, until butter is fragrant and browned, about 1 minute. Stir in shallots and garlic; cook, stirring, until fragrant, about 1 minute.

Stir in carrots; cook, stirring, just until beginning to soften, about 2 minutes. Stir in snow peas; cook, stirring, until carrots and snow peas are tender-crisp, about 2 minutes. Stir in shrimp, salt and pepper. Serve with lemon wedges.

TIP FROM THE TEST KITCHEN
Keep a close eye on the butter as it's browning, as it can burn quickly. If it blackens, simply scrape out the skillet and start again with new butter.

NUTRITIONAL INFORMATION, PER SERVING: about 183 cal, 19 g pro, 7 g total fat (4 g sat. fat), 10 g carb, 3 g fibre, 144 mg chol, 336 mg sodium, 394 mg potassium. % RDI: 8% calcium, 23% iron, 86% vit A, 40% vit C, 12% folate.

Serve this scampi over pasta or rice, or with crusty bread.

Spot Prawn Scampi

HANDS-ON TIME
15 MINUTES

TOTAL TIME
15 MINUTES

MAKES
4 SERVINGS

What you need

450 g	spot prawns (see tip, below), peeled and deveined
¼ tsp	each salt and pepper
2 tsp	olive oil
4	cloves garlic, minced
¼ tsp	hot pepper flakes
½ cup	dry white wine
2 tbsp	butter
¼ tsp	grated lemon zest
2 tbsp	lemon juice
3 tbsp	chopped fresh parsley
2 tbsp	chopped fresh tarragon or fresh parsley
	lemon wedges (optional)

How to make it

Sprinkle prawns with salt and pepper. In large nonstick skillet, heat oil over medium-high heat; sauté prawns until opaque throughout, about 2 minutes. Using slotted spoon, transfer to plate. Set aside.

Return skillet to medium-high heat; cook garlic and hot pepper flakes, stirring, until fragrant, about 1 minute. Add wine; cook, stirring often, until reduced by half, about 3 minutes. Add butter; cook, swirling skillet, until melted. Stir in lemon zest and lemon juice; cook for 1 minute.

Stir in prawns, 2 tbsp of the parsley and 1 tbsp of the tarragon. Sprinkle with remaining parsley and tarragon. Serve with lemon wedges (if using).

TIP FROM THE TEST KITCHEN

Sweet, tender wild spot prawns from British Columbia are in season from about May through July, and are a sustainable alternative to imported shrimp. During the off-season, substitute large prawns or shrimp certified by the Aquaculture Stewardship Council (ASC). You can use frozen spot prawns, but they tend to turn mushy when thawed.

NUTRITIONAL INFORMATION, PER SERVING: about 179 cal, 17 g pro, 9 g total fat (4 g sat. fat), 3 g carb, trace fibre, 137 mg chol, 306 mg sodium, 217 mg potassium. % RDI: 5% calcium, 16% iron, 11% vit A, 15% vit C, 5% folate.

Beer-Battered Pickerel

HANDS-ON TIME	TOTAL TIME	MAKES
30 MINUTES	40 MINUTES	8 SERVINGS

What you need

3⅓ cups	all-purpose flour
1¾ tsp	salt
½ tsp	cayenne pepper
2	bottles (each 341 mL) beer
	vegetable oil for frying
900 g	skinless pickerel fillets
8	lemon wedges

How to make it

In large bowl, whisk together 3 cups of the flour, the salt and cayenne pepper; whisk in beer until smooth. Let stand for 15 minutes.

Pour enough oil into deep fryer or large deep heavy-bottomed saucepan to come no more than halfway up side; heat until deep-fryer thermometer reads 375°F (190°C).

Meanwhile, cut fish into serving-size pieces. Spread remaining flour in shallow dish; dredge fish in flour, shaking off excess. Dip into batter to coat. Deep-fry fish, turning once, until golden brown, 6 to 8 minutes.

Using slotted spoon, transfer fish to paper towel–lined rimmed baking sheet; let drain. Serve with lemon wedges.

TIP FROM THE TEST KITCHEN
Mix the batter in a deep bowl to make dipping and coating the fillets easy.

NUTRITIONAL INFORMATION, PER SERVING: about 389 cal, 25 g pro, 20 g total fat (2 g sat. fat), 23 g carb, 1 g fibre, 98 mg chol, 340 mg sodium, 491 mg potassium. % RDI: 12% calcium, 20% iron, 3% vit A, 5% vit C, 29% folate.

Shore Lunch—Style Fried Whitefish

HANDS-ON TIME	•	TOTAL TIME	•	MAKES
30 MINUTES		30 MINUTES		6 SERVINGS

What you need

½ cup	whole wheat flour
¼ cup	cornmeal
1 tsp	salt-free lemon-pepper seasoning (such as Mrs. Dash)
1 tsp	salt
¾ tsp	sweet paprika
	vegetable oil for frying
675 g	skinless whitefish fillets (see tip, below), cut crosswise in 1-inch (2.5 cm) wide strips
	lemon wedges

How to make it

In pie plate or shallow dish, whisk together flour, cornmeal, lemon-pepper seasoning, salt and paprika.

Pour enough oil into wok or large deep heavy-bottomed saucepan to come 1 inch (2.5 cm) up side; heat until deep-fryer thermometer reads 375°F (190°C).

Dredge fish in flour mixture, turning to coat; shake off excess. Working in batches, deep-fry fish, turning once, until golden, about 4 minutes.

Using slotted spoon, transfer to paper towel—lined baking sheet; let drain. Serve with lemon wedges.

TIP FROM THE TEST KITCHEN

For this recipe and the one on the opposite page, use the freshest firm, white-fleshed fish you can find. Pickerel, whitefish, halibut and cod are all delicious options.

NUTRITIONAL INFORMATION, PER SERVING: about 178 cal, 22 g pro, 8 g total fat (1 g sat. fat), 4 g carb, 1 g fibre, 68 mg chol, 173 mg sodium, 380 mg potassium. % RDI: 3% calcium, 4% iron, 5% vit A, 3% folate.

Broiled Devilled Halibut

HANDS-ON TIME		TOTAL TIME		MAKES
15 MINUTES	•	15 MINUTES	•	4 SERVINGS

What you need

4	pieces skinless halibut fillet (each about 115 g)
1 tbsp	Dijon or hot mustard
1 tbsp	fresh tarragon leaves (or 1 tsp dried tarragon)
4	thin slices prosciutto (each about 30 g) or other ham
pinch	pepper
2 tsp	olive oil

How to make it

Brush both sides of fish with mustard; sprinkle with tarragon. Wrap 1 prosciutto slice around each piece; sprinkle both sides with pepper. Brush with oil.

Place fish, prosciutto seam side down, on foil-lined broiler pan; broil, turning once, until fish flakes easily when tested, about 3 minutes per side.

NUTRITIONAL INFORMATION, PER SERVING: about 193 cal, 29 g pro, 8 g total fat (2 g sat. fat), 1 g carb, trace fibre, 51 mg chol, 474 mg sodium, 602 mg potassium. % RDI: 6% calcium, 9% iron, 5% vit A, 6% folate.

A bed of steamed asparagus makes a tasty base for this salty, tangy fish.

Grill extra lemon halves if you like a bit more citrus juice on your fish.

Grilled Lemon Herb Trout for Two

HANDS-ON TIME	TOTAL TIME	MAKES
15 MINUTES	15 MINUTES	2 SERVINGS

What you need

1	whole trout, cleaned (about 900 g), see tip, below
½ tsp	each salt and pepper
1	lemon, halved
2	bay leaves
10	sprigs fresh parsley
2	sprigs fresh thyme
1 tbsp	extra-virgin olive oil

How to make it

Sprinkle inside of fish with ¼ tsp each of the salt and pepper. Cut 1 lemon half into slices; stuff lemon slices, bay leaves, parsley and thyme into fish cavity.

Rub 1½ tsp of the oil all over outside of fish; sprinkle with remaining salt and pepper.

Place fish and remaining lemon half on well-greased grill over medium-high heat; close lid and grill, turning once, until fish flakes easily when tested, about 10 minutes per side.

Transfer to serving platter. Squeeze grilled lemon over top; drizzle with remaining oil.

TIP FROM THE TEST KITCHEN

A cleaned fish usually has the fins, scales and innards removed. Most whole fish are sold already cleaned. If you find one that isn't, just ask your fishmonger to do it for you.

NUTRITIONAL INFORMATION, PER SERVING: about 488 cal, 61 g pro, 25 g total fat (6 g sat. fat), 2 g carb, trace fibre, 170 mg chol, 679 mg sodium, 1,134 mg potassium. % RDI: 20% calcium, 7% iron, 22% vit A, 32% vit C, 29% folate.

Pickerel and Potato Packets

HANDS-ON TIME	•	TOTAL TIME	•	MAKES
15 MINUTES		35 MINUTES		4 SERVINGS

What you need

3 tbsp	extra-virgin olive oil
2 tbsp	lemon juice
1 tbsp	chopped fresh parsley
2 tsp	chopped fresh dill
½ tsp	each salt and pepper
340 g	yellow-fleshed potatoes (unpeeled), sliced paper-thin crosswise (see tip, below)
1	small onion, thinly sliced
675 g	skinless pickerel fillets, cut in 4 pieces

How to make it

Whisk together 2 tbsp of the oil, the lemon juice, parsley, dill and ¼ tsp each of the salt and pepper; set aside.

In bowl, toss together potatoes, onion and remaining oil, salt and pepper. Divide among 4 large squares of double-thickness foil. Top each with 1 piece of the fish; drizzle with lemon mixture. Fold foil over loosely, leaving airspace above fish for steam; seal edges to form packets.

Place packets on grill over medium-high heat; close lid and grill until potatoes are tender and fish flakes easily when tested, 12 to 15 minutes.

TIP FROM THE TEST KITCHEN

Use a mandoline to cut paper-thin potato slices. Or substitute cooked whole potatoes that have been cut into thicker slices; both need the same amount of time to cook on the grill.

NUTRITIONAL INFORMATION, PER SERVING: about 320 cal, 35 g pro, 12 g total fat (2 g sat. fat), 17 g carb, 2 g fibre, 146 mg chol, 383 mg sodium, 1,138 mg potassium. % RDI: 19% calcium, 26% iron, 4% vit A, 27% vit C, 11% folate.

Rainbow Trout With Dijon Mayonnaise

HANDS-ON TIME	TOTAL TIME	MAKES
10 MINUTES	10 MINUTES	4 SERVINGS

What you need

4	rainbow trout fillets (each about 170 g), see tip, below
2 tbsp	light mayonnaise
2 tsp	Dijon mustard
¼ tsp	each salt and pepper
1 tbsp	chopped fresh parsley
	lemon wedges

How to make it

Pat fish dry; place on greased rimmed baking sheet. Stir together mayonnaise, mustard, salt and pepper; spread over fish.

Broil fish, 6 inches (15 cm) from heat, until fish flakes easily when tested, about 6 minutes.

Transfer fish to serving plates; sprinkle with parsley. Serve with lemon wedges.

VARIATIONS

Rainbow Trout With Indian Curry Mayonnaise
Replace mustard with 2 tsp mild Indian curry paste.

Rainbow Trout With Thai Red Curry Mayonnaise
Replace mustard with 1 tsp Thai red curry paste.

TIP FROM THE TEST KITCHEN
This recipe works equally well with skin-on or skinless rainbow trout fillets. If you're using skin-on, broil the fish skin side down.

NUTRITIONAL INFORMATION, PER SERVING: about 226 cal, 29 g pro, 11 g total fat (3 g sat. fat), 1 g carb, 0 g fibre, 82 mg chol, 282 mg sodium. % RDI: 10% calcium, 4% iron, 11% vit A, 13% vit C, 14% folate.

Grilled Mango Scallop Skewers With Spinach Toss

HANDS-ON TIME	•	TOTAL TIME	•	MAKES
15 MINUTES		15 MINUTES		4 SERVINGS

What you need

MANGO SCALLOP SKEWERS:

24	large sea scallops (720 g)
1	mango, peeled, pitted and cut in sixteen ¾-inch (2 cm) cubes
2 tbsp	butter, melted
2 tsp	Dijon mustard

SPINACH TOSS:

6 cups	baby spinach
1	sweet red pepper, cut in matchsticks
⅓ cup	matchstick-cut peeled pitted mango
¼ cup	thinly sliced red onion
2 tbsp	olive oil
2 tsp	lemon juice
1 tsp	Dijon mustard
pinch	each salt and pepper

How to make it

MANGO SCALLOP SKEWERS: Alternately thread 3 scallops and 2 mango cubes onto each of 8 metal or soaked wooden skewers.

Gradually whisk butter with mustard; brush half over 1 side of the skewers. Place, buttered side down, on greased grill over medium-high heat; close lid and grill for 2 minutes. Brush with remaining butter mixture; turn and grill until scallops are opaque throughout, about 2 minutes.

SPINACH TOSS: While skewers are grilling, combine spinach, red pepper, mango and red onion; arrange on serving platter. Whisk together oil, lemon juice, mustard, salt and pepper; drizzle over salad. Top with Mango Scallop Skewers.

VARIATION

Baked Mango Scallop Skewers With Spinach Toss

Bake skewers on greased foil-lined rimmed baking sheet in 400°F (200°C) oven, turning once, until scallops are opaque throughout, about 4 minutes.

NUTRITIONAL INFORMATION, PER SERVING: about 249 cal, 17 g pro, 14 g total fat (5 g sat. fat), 16 g carb, 3 g fibre, 49 mg chol, 294 mg sodium, 735 mg potassium. % RDI: 12% calcium, 25% iron, 62% vit A, 108% vit C, 53% folate.

To prevent charring, soak wooden skewers in water for 30 minutes to 1 hour before you grill.

Salmon Kabobs With Baby Bok Choy

HANDS-ON TIME	•	TOTAL TIME	•	MAKES
30 MINUTES		30 MINUTES		4 SERVINGS

What you need

SALMON KABOBS:

4 tsp	soy sauce
1 tbsp	oyster sauce
2 tsp	each lemon juice and sesame oil
1 tsp	liquid honey
¼ tsp	hot pepper flakes
4	skinless salmon fillets (each 170 g), quartered crosswise

BABY BOK CHOY:

1 tbsp	butter
1	shallot, minced
2 tsp	minced fresh ginger
1	clove garlic, minced
4	baby bok choy, halved lengthwise
¼ tsp	salt
1 tsp	sesame oil

How to make it

SALMON KABOBS: In baking dish, whisk together soy sauce, oyster sauce, lemon juice, sesame oil, honey and hot pepper flakes. Add fish, turning to coat; let stand for 10 minutes.

Thread fish onto metal or soaked wooden skewers. Place on greased grill over medium-high heat; close lid and grill until grill-marked and fish flakes easily when tested, 8 to 10 minutes.

BABY BOK CHOY: While kabobs are grilling, in skillet, melt butter over medium-high heat; sauté shallot, ginger and garlic for 1 minute. Add bok choy, salt and ¼ cup water; cover and steam for 2 minutes. Uncover and cook until tender-crisp, 2 to 3 minutes. Drizzle with sesame oil. Serve with Salmon Kabobs.

TIP FROM THE TEST KITCHEN
Serve the kabobs with hot cooked brown, wild or white rice. If your bok choy heads are tiny, use double the number called for in the ingredient list.

NUTRITIONAL INFORMATION, PER SERVING: about 338 cal, 31 g pro, 22 g total fat (6 g sat. fat), 4 g carb, 1 g fibre, 91 mg chol, 483 mg sodium, 835 mg potassium. % RDI: 9% calcium, 10% iron, 39% vit A, 43% vit C, 36% folate.

Grilled Salmon Fillets

| HANDS-ON TIME | • | TOTAL TIME | • | MAKES |
| 15 MINUTES | | 45 MINUTES | | 4 SERVINGS |

What you need

⅓ cup	olive oil
1 tsp	grated lemon zest
¼ cup	lemon juice
2 tbsp	chopped fresh dill
¼ tsp	each salt and pepper
4	skin-on salmon fillets (each about 250 g)

How to make it

In shallow dish, whisk together oil, lemon zest, lemon juice, dill, salt and pepper; add fish, turning to coat. Cover and refrigerate, turning occasionally, for up to 30 minutes.

Remove fish from marinade, reserving remainder. Place fish, skin side down, on greased grill over medium-high heat; close lid and grill, turning once and basting frequently with reserved marinade, just until opaque throughout and fish flakes easily when tested, about 10 minutes per each 1 inch (2.5 cm) of thickness.

TIP FROM THE TEST KITCHEN
Be gentle when turning the fish; it's best to use two spatulas, placing one under and one over each fillet.

NUTRITIONAL INFORMATION, PER SERVING: about 341 cal, 19 g pro, 29 g total fat (5 g sat. fat), 2 g carb, trace fibre, 54 mg chol, 197 mg sodium, 355 mg potassium. % RDI: 1% calcium, 4% iron, 2% vit A, 18% vit C, 15% folate.

For grilling, choose thick skin-on fillets—they hold together better.

Try the charmoulah as a dipping sauce, condiment or marinade. It's delish with chicken, lamb, pork and veggies.

Grilled Pickerel With Charmoulah

HANDS-ON TIME	•	TOTAL TIME	•	MAKES
20 MINUTES		20 MINUTES		4 SERVINGS

What you need

CHARMOULAH:

½ cup	chopped fresh parsley
½ cup	chopped fresh cilantro
2	green onions, finely chopped
¼ cup	extra-virgin olive oil
3 tbsp	lemon juice
2	cloves garlic, minced
1 tsp	ground cumin
1 tsp	sweet paprika
¼ tsp	cayenne pepper
¼ tsp	each salt and pepper

GRILLED PICKEREL:

675 g	skin-on pickerel, perch or other freshwater fish fillets
¼ tsp	each salt and pepper

How to make it

CHARMOULAH: Stir together parsley, cilantro, green onions, oil, lemon juice, garlic, cumin, paprika, cayenne pepper, salt and pepper. Set aside.

GRILLED PICKEREL: Divide fish into 4 portions. Using 2 metal or soaked wooden skewers per portion, skewer fish crosswise; sprinkle with salt and pepper.

Place fish, skin side down, on greased grill over medium-high heat; close lid and grill, turning once, until fish flakes easily when tested, about 5 minutes per each ½ inch (1 cm) of thickness. Serve topped with Charmoulah.

TIP FROM THE TEST KITCHEN
Pickerel (often called walleye) is an excellent, sustainable fish choice. Its flaky white flesh has a pleasing, mild flavour.

NUTRITIONAL INFORMATION, PER SERVING: about 274 cal, 30 g pro, 16 g total fat (2 g sat. fat), 3 g carb, 1 g fibre, 129 mg chol, 374 mg sodium. % RDI: 18% calcium, 24% iron, 15% vit A, 27% vit C, 18% folate.

Lemon-Basil Tilapia
With Charred Tomatoes and Zucchini Wedges

HANDS-ON TIME	TOTAL TIME	MAKES
25 MINUTES	25 MINUTES	4 SERVINGS

What you need

1 tbsp	olive oil
1 tbsp	chopped fresh basil
½ tsp	grated lemon zest
½ tsp	each salt and pepper
300 g	skinless tilapia fillets (about 2 large), halved lengthwise
4	zucchini, quartered lengthwise and seeded
4	plum tomatoes, halved lengthwise
2 tsp	balsamic vinegar
2 tbsp	grated Parmesan cheese

How to make it

Stir together 1 tsp of the oil, 1½ tsp of the basil, the lemon zest and ¼ tsp each of the salt and pepper; rub all over fish. Set aside.

In bowl, toss together zucchini, 1 tsp of the remaining oil and a pinch each of the remaining salt and pepper. In separate bowl, toss together tomatoes, vinegar and remaining oil, salt and pepper.

Place zucchini and tomatoes on greased grill over medium-high heat; close lid and grill, turning occasionally, until zucchini is tender and tomatoes are softened, about 10 minutes. Transfer to separate plates; sprinkle zucchini with Parmesan and sprinkle tomatoes with remaining basil. Keep warm.

Meanwhile, place fish on greased grill; close lid and grill, turning once, until fish flakes easily when tested, 6 to 8 minutes. Serve with zucchini and tomatoes.

TIP FROM THE TEST KITCHEN
In place of the tilapia, you can substitute any firm-fleshed fish that will hold its shape on a hot, well-oiled grill, such as cod or halibut.

NUTRITIONAL INFORMATION, PER SERVING: about 154 cal, 19 g pro, 7 g total fat (2 g sat. fat), 7 g carb, 2 g fibre, 36 mg chol, 376 mg sodium, 764 mg potassium. % RDI: 7% calcium, 9% iron, 22% vit A, 45% vit C, 23% folate.

Jamaican Jerk Trout

HANDS-ON TIME	•	TOTAL TIME	•	MAKES
10 MINUTES		15 MINUTES		4 SERVINGS

What you need

1 tbsp	vegetable oil
1 tbsp	lime juice
1	green onion, minced
1	jalapeño pepper, seeded and minced
1	clove garlic, grated or pressed
1 tsp	dried thyme
1 tsp	ground allspice
½ tsp	salt
¼ tsp	ground ginger
¼ tsp	pepper
¼ tsp	granulated sugar
pinch	cinnamon
pinch	nutmeg
4	skin-on trout fillets (each about 170 g)

How to make it

Stir together oil, lime juice, green onion, jalapeño, garlic, thyme, allspice, salt, ginger, pepper, sugar, cinnamon and nutmeg.

Arrange fish, skin side down, on foil-lined rimmed baking sheet; brush oil mixture over fleshy side. Broil, 6 inches (15 cm) from heat, until fish flakes easily when tested, 6 to 10 minutes.

NUTRITIONAL INFORMATION, PER SERVING: about 237 cal, 29 g pro, 12 g total fat (3 g sat. fat), 2 g carb, 1 g fibre, 80 mg chol, 338 mg sodium, 555 mg potassium. % RDI: 10% calcium, 6% iron, 11% vit A, 10% vit C, 15% folate.

Tomato and Garlic Steamed Mussels

HANDS-ON TIME	•	TOTAL TIME	•	MAKES
20 MINUTES		25 MINUTES		4 SERVINGS

What you need

900 g	mussels (see tip, below)
1 tbsp	olive oil
1	shallot, sliced
4	cloves garlic, sliced
1½ cups	tomato-based pasta sauce
¾ cup	dry white wine
2 tbsp	chopped fresh parsley
1 tsp	chopped fresh tarragon

How to make it

Scrub mussels; remove any beards. Discard any mussels that do not close when tapped. Set aside.

In Dutch oven or large heavy-bottomed saucepan, heat oil over medium heat; cook shallot and garlic, stirring occasionally, until softened and golden, about 5 minutes.

Stir in pasta sauce and wine; bring to simmer. Add mussels; cover with tight-fitting lid. Cook until mussels open, about 5 minutes. Discard any mussels that do not open. Remove from heat; stir in parsley and tarragon.

TIP FROM THE TEST KITCHEN

Most mussels today are suspension cultured, meaning they perch on a rope suspended from a buoy. As a result, they are fairly clean and need minimal rinsing. Just pull off any visible beards, seaweed or shell bits sticking out from the edges.

NUTRITIONAL INFORMATION, PER SERVING: about 221 cal, 13 g pro, 8 g total fat (2 g sat. fat), 18 g carb, 3 g fibre, 28 mg chol, 562 mg sodium, 489 mg potassium. % RDI: 4% calcium, 30% iron, 13% vit A, 18% vit C, 21% folate.

To store mussels before cooking, place them in a bowl in the back of your fridge and cover with a damp cloth. They will keep for up to two days.

Asian Fish
en Papillote
opposite

Asian Fish en Papillote

What you need

4	skinless sole or tilapia fillets
¼ tsp	each salt and pepper
4 tsp	matchstick-cut fresh ginger
4 tsp	vegetable oil
4 tsp	black bean garlic sauce
2 tsp	unseasoned rice vinegar
1	clove garlic, minced
1	red or green finger chili pepper (optional), thinly sliced
half	onion, thinly sliced
3 tbsp	fresh cilantro leaves

How to make it

Sprinkle fish with salt and pepper. In large bowl, stir together ginger, oil, black bean sauce, vinegar, garlic, chili pepper (if using) and onion. Add fish, turning to coat. Cover and refrigerate, turning once, for 20 minutes.

Meanwhile, cut four 15-inch (38 cm) squares of parchment paper; fold each in half. Open paper; place 1 of the fish fillets on 1 side of each piece. Fold paper over so edges meet; double-fold edges and seal to form packets.

Bake on rimmed baking sheet in 400°F (200°C) oven until fish flakes easily when tested, about 10 minutes. Open packets; sprinkle fish with cilantro.

NUTRITIONAL INFORMATION, PER SERVING: about 210 cal, 31 g pro, 7 g total fat (1 g sat. fat), 5 g carb, 1 g fibre, 78 mg chol, 336 mg sodium, 647 mg potassium. % RDI: 4% calcium, 7% iron, 2% vit A, 5% vit C, 7% folate.

Coconut-Poached Halibut With Broccolini

What you need

2 tsp	vegetable oil
3	cloves garlic, minced
2 tsp	grated fresh ginger
1	can (400 mL) coconut milk
¾ tsp	Thai green curry paste
4	skin-on halibut fillets (450 g total)
1 tbsp	lime juice
pinch	each salt and pepper
450 g	Broccolini, trimmed
½ cup	chopped fresh cilantro
1	hot red pepper (optional), such as Thai bird's-eye, thinly sliced

How to make it

In large skillet, heat oil over medium heat; cook garlic and ginger, stirring, until fragrant, about 2 minutes. Stir in coconut milk and curry paste; bring to boil. Reduce heat to medium-low; add fish and cook, turning once, until fish flakes easily when tested, about 4 minutes per side. Remove skin. Transfer fish to serving platter; keep warm.

Simmer sauce over medium-low heat until thick enough to coat back of spoon, about 7 minutes. Stir in lime juice, salt and pepper. Ladle over fish.

While sauce is simmering, in large saucepan of boiling salted water, cook Broccolini until tender-crisp, about 5 minutes. Drain; arrange on plate with fish. Sprinkle with cilantro, and hot pepper (if using).

NUTRITIONAL INFORMATION, PER SERVING: about 375 cal, 28 g pro, 25 g total fat (19 g sat. fat), 12 g carb, 2 g fibre, 33 mg chol, 410 mg sodium, 1,064 mg potassium. % RDI: 14% calcium, 36% iron, 25% vit A, 127% vit C, 35% folate.

Tomato and Fennel Poached Tilapia

HANDS-ON TIME	TOTAL TIME	MAKES
30 MINUTES	30 MINUTES	4 SERVINGS

What you need

1	bulb fennel
1 tbsp	olive oil
1	onion, thinly sliced
1 tsp	fennel seeds, crushed
pinch	hot pepper flakes
1	bottle (680 mL) strained tomatoes (passata)
450 g	skinless tilapia fillets (about 2), quartered
½ tsp	salt
¼ tsp	pepper
1 cup	whole wheat couscous
1¼ cups	boiling water
1 tbsp	chopped fresh tarragon

How to make it

Reserving fronds, trim fennel; quarter lengthwise and remove core. Thinly slice fennel lengthwise.

In large skillet, heat oil over medium heat; cook sliced fennel, onion, fennel seeds and hot pepper flakes, stirring, until sliced fennel is softened, about 10 minutes.

Stir in strained tomatoes and ¼ cup water; bring to boil. Reduce heat and simmer for 5 minutes.

Sprinkle fish with salt and pepper; add to fennel mixture. Cover and cook over medium-low heat until fish flakes easily when tested, about 8 minutes.

While fish is cooking, place couscous in heatproof bowl; pour in boiling water. Cover and let stand until no liquid remains, about 10 minutes. Fluff with fork.

Serve couscous topped with fish and sauce; sprinkle with tarragon and reserved fennel fronds.

NUTRITIONAL INFORMATION, PER SERVING: about 388 cal, 31 g pro, 7 g total fat (1 g sat. fat), 52 g carb, 8 g fibre, 57 mg chol, 721 mg sodium, 1,044 mg potassium. % RDI: 8% calcium, 42% iron, 1% vit A, 17% vit C, 25% folate.

Poached Salmon With Salsa Verde

HANDS-ON TIME		TOTAL TIME		MAKES
15 MINUTES	•	20 MINUTES	•	4 SERVINGS

What you need

POACHED SALMON:

1	onion, thinly sliced
1	rib celery, thinly sliced
3	thin slices lemon
4	sprigs fresh parsley
½ tsp	each salt and black peppercorns
4	skin-on salmon fillets (each 175 g)

SALSA VERDE:

⅓ cup	fresh bread crumbs
3 tbsp	red wine vinegar
1	hard-cooked egg, coarsely chopped
1	bunch fresh parsley, stemmed
2 tbsp	capers, drained and rinsed
2	anchovy fillets
1	clove garlic
¼ cup	extra-virgin olive oil
4	lemon wedges

How to make it

POACHED SALMON: In wide shallow pan large enough to hold fish in single layer, bring onion, celery, lemon, parsley, salt, peppercorns and 3 cups water to boil. Cover, reduce heat and simmer for 5 minutes.

Add fish; cover and poach just below simmer just until fish flakes easily when tested, 5 to 7 minutes. Using slotted spatula, transfer fish to plates; remove skin. Reserve 3 tbsp of the poaching liquid for Salsa Verde.

SALSA VERDE: While onion mixture is simmering, soak bread crumbs in vinegar for 5 minutes; transfer to food processor. Add egg, parsley, capers, anchovies and garlic; pulse until finely chopped. With motor running, drizzle in oil and reserved poaching liquid.

TO FINISH: Serve Poached Salmon with Salsa Verde and lemon wedges.

NUTRITIONAL INFORMATION, PER SERVING: about 476 cal, 37 g pro, 34 g total fat (6 g sat. fat), 4 g carb, 1 g fibre, 149 mg chol, 562 mg sodium, 702 mg potassium. % RDI: 7% calcium, 19% iron, 25% vit A, 65% vit C, 38% folate.

Steamed Pickerel
With Oyster Mushroom Sauce

HANDS-ON TIME	TOTAL TIME	MAKES
15 MINUTES	25 MINUTES	4 SERVINGS

What you need

565 g	skin-on pickerel fillets (see tip, below), cut in 4 portions
¼ tsp	salt
pinch	white or black pepper
340 g	oyster mushrooms
3	green onions
2 tbsp	soy sauce
2 tbsp	Chinese rice wine, dry sherry or sake
2 tsp	minced fresh ginger
⅓ cup	sodium-reduced chicken broth
2 tsp	cornstarch
1 tsp	sesame oil

How to make it

In 10-inch (25 cm) pie plate, arrange fish flesh side up; sprinkle with salt and pepper.

Trim off hard ends of mushroom stems; tear large mushrooms into 2 or 3 pieces, leaving small ones whole. Keeping white and green parts separate, thinly slice green onions. Toss together mushrooms, white parts of green onions, soy sauce, wine and ginger; spoon over fish.

Place rack insert in wok; pour in enough water to come 1 inch (2.5 cm) below rack. Bring water to boil. Place pie plate on rack; cover and steam fish mixture over high heat until fish flakes easily when tested and mushrooms are tender, 10 to 15 minutes.

Pour juices in pie plate into small saucepan. Whisk chicken broth with cornstarch; stir into pan and bring to boil. Reduce heat and simmer for 1 minute. Stir in sesame oil and green parts of green onions. Serve sauce over fish and mushrooms.

TIP FROM THE TEST KITCHEN
Skin-on fillets hold together better during steaming. If you're not a fan of eating fish skin, no problem; it's easy to peel off and discard after cooking.

NUTRITIONAL INFORMATION, PER SERVING: about 186 cal, 30 g pro, 3 g total fat (1 g sat. fat), 8 g carb, 2 g fibre, 122 mg chol, 730 mg sodium, 883 mg potassium. % RDI: 15% calcium, 22% iron, 4% vit A, 2% vit C, 12% folate.

Boiled Lobster
With Lemon-Anchovy Butter

HANDS-ON TIME	TOTAL TIME	MAKES
15 MINUTES	25 MINUTES	4 SERVINGS

What you need

LEMON-ANCHOVY BUTTER:

⅓ cup	butter, softened
2 tsp	chopped fresh parsley
1	clove garlic, grated
1	anchovy fillet, minced
½ tsp	grated lemon zest
¼ tsp	lemon juice

BOILED LOBSTER:

4	live lobsters (each 565 to 675 g)

How to make it

LEMON-ANCHOVY BUTTER: In bowl, mash together butter, parsley, garlic, anchovy, lemon zest and lemon juice. Set aside. *(Make-ahead: Cover and refrigerate for up to 3 days or freeze in airtight container for up to 2 months.)*

BOILED LOBSTER: Fill stockpot with enough salted water to completely cover lobsters when immersed; bring to full rolling boil over high heat. Grasp each lobster around back shell, snip off elastic bands and gently drop headfirst into water. Cover and return to boil, starting timer when water boils.

Reduce heat to slow boil; cook lobsters until bright red and small leg comes away easily when twisted and pulled, 8 to 10 minutes.

TO FINISH: While lobsters are boiling, in saucepan, melt Lemon-Anchovy Butter over low heat. Serve with lobster for dipping.

How to Crack a Lobster

1 Twist off each claw at body joint; twist apart claw and arm sections. Break off small part of each claw and remove meat with lobster pick or nut pick. Grab large part of each claw around notch; bend in half to split open. Lift out meat. Crack each arm; pick out meat.

2 With fingers or fork, pry tail out of shell; pick out meat from flippers.

3 Eat red coral (if any) and green tomalley, if desired. Pick out meat from body. Break off legs; suck out juice and meat.

NUTRITIONAL INFORMATION, PER SERVING: about 282 cal, 31 g pro, 16 g total fat (10 g sat. fat), 2 g carb, trace fibre, 147 mg chol, 702 mg sodium, 532 mg potassium. % RDI: 9% calcium, 5% iron, 18% vit A, 2% vit C, 7% folate.

Change up your lobster feast!

The tasty variations below are pictured right (top to bottom).

....

Boiled Lobster With Lemony Dill Butter

Omit Lemon-Anchovy Butter. Mash together ⅓ cup butter, softened; 2 tbsp chopped fresh dill; and 1 tsp grated lemon zest. Melt as directed while lobsters are cooking.

Boiled Lobster With Spicy Garlic Butter

Omit Lemon-Anchovy Butter. In small skillet, melt 2 tsp butter over medium heat. Cook 3 cloves garlic, minced; and ½ tsp smoked paprika, stirring, until garlic is softened, about 2 minutes. Transfer to bowl; let cool to room temperature, about 5 minutes. Mash in ⅓ cup butter, softened; and 1 tsp hot pepper sauce. Melt as directed while lobsters are cooking.

Boiled Lobster With Curried Ginger Butter

Omit Lemon-Anchovy Butter. In small skillet, melt 2 tsp butter over medium heat. Cook 2 tbsp minced green onion, 1 tsp minced fresh ginger and ½ tsp curry powder, stirring, until ginger is softened, about 3 minutes. Transfer to bowl; let cool to room temperature, about 5 minutes. Mash in ⅓ cup butter, softened. Melt as directed while lobsters are cooking.

Boiled Lobster With Zesty Mayo

Omit Lemon-Anchovy Butter. Stir together ⅓ cup mayonnaise, 2 tbsp finely chopped fresh chives, 1 tsp grainy mustard and pinch cayenne pepper. Serve with lobsters.

Chinese-Style Steamed Fish and Sesame Broccoli

HANDS-ON TIME	•	TOTAL TIME	•	MAKES
10 MINUTES		25 MINUTES		4 SERVINGS

What you need

STEAMED FISH:

565 g	skin-on firm white fish fillets (such as pickerel, cod or halibut)
2 tbsp	matchstick-cut fresh ginger
2 tbsp	sodium-reduced soy sauce
1 tbsp	lemon juice
2 tsp	sesame oil
2	green onions, cut in thin strips (white and green parts separated)

SESAME BROCCOLI:

1 tbsp	vegetable oil
2 tsp	sesame oil
1	clove garlic, thinly sliced
1	head broccoli, cut in florets
1 tbsp	sesame seeds, toasted

How to make it

STEAMED FISH: In 10-inch (25 cm) pie plate, arrange fish, skin side down; sprinkle with ginger, soy sauce, lemon juice and sesame oil. Arrange white parts of green onions on top.

Place rack insert in wok; pour in enough water to come 1 inch (2.5 cm) below rack. Bring to boil. Place pie plate on rack; cover and steam over high heat until fish flakes easily when tested, 10 to 12 minutes. Top with green parts of green onions. Spoon pan juices over fish.

SESAME BROCCOLI: While fish is steaming, in wok or large skillet, heat vegetable oil and sesame oil over medium-high heat; stir-fry garlic for 30 seconds. Add broccoli; stir-fry for 1 minute. Add ¼ cup water; cover and steam until tender, about 4 minutes. Sprinkle with sesame seeds. Serve with Steamed Fish.

NUTRITIONAL INFORMATION, PER SERVING: about 254 cal, 28 g pro, 11 g total fat (2 g sat. fat), 11 g carb, 3 g fibre, 108 mg chol, 414 mg sodium, 899 mg potassium. % RDI: 18% calcium, 21% iron, 21% vit A, 127% vit C, 67% folate.

Beer-Steamed Clams

HANDS-ON TIME	TOTAL TIME	MAKES
20 MINUTES	25 MINUTES	4 SERVINGS

What you need

4	strips thick-sliced bacon, chopped
2	shallots, diced
half	sweet red pepper, diced
3	cloves garlic, minced
1 cup	wheat beer or pale ale
1.8 kg	littleneck clams, scrubbed
2 tbsp	chopped fresh parsley

How to make it

In Dutch oven, cook bacon over medium heat, stirring often, until crisp, about 6 minutes. Using slotted spoon, transfer to paper towel–lined plate; let drain.

Drain all but 1 tsp fat from pan; cook shallots, red pepper and garlic, stirring occasionally, until softened, about 3 minutes.

Add beer and bring to boil over high heat. Add clams; cover and boil until clams open, about 7 minutes.

Transfer clams to large bowl, discarding any that do not open; pour cooking liquid over top. Sprinkle with bacon and parsley.

NUTRITIONAL INFORMATION, PER SERVING: about 132 cal, 12 g pro, 5 g total fat (2 g sat. fat), 6 g carb, trace fibre, 32 mg chol, 228 mg sodium, 333 mg potassium. % RDI: 4% calcium, 71% iron, 13% vit A, 58% vit C, 9% folate.

Calamari in Tomato White Wine Sauce

HANDS-ON TIME	TOTAL TIME	MAKES
20 MINUTES	30 MINUTES	4 SERVINGS

What you need

450 g	whole squid
2 tbsp	olive oil
half	onion, thinly sliced
1	clove garlic, thinly sliced
½ cup	dry white wine
¼ tsp	hot pepper flakes
1½ cups	chopped seeded drained canned whole tomatoes
¼ tsp	salt

How to make it

Holding each squid tube, pull off head and tentacles; set aside. Rinse tubes under cold water, rubbing off purplish skin. Pull out and discard "pen" (clear long plastic-like skeleton) from centre of each tube. Pull off and discard fins from tubes.

Cut off and discard eyes and head from tentacles, keeping tentacles attached to ring on top; squeeze hard beak from centre of tentacles and discard. Cut tubes crosswise into ½-inch (1 cm) wide rings; pat dry. Set aside.

In saucepan, heat oil over medium heat; cook onion and garlic, stirring occasionally, until softened, about 3 minutes. Add wine and hot pepper flakes; cook for 1 minute. Add tomatoes; bring to boil. Reduce heat and simmer for 5 minutes. Add squid; simmer until tender, about 5 minutes. Sprinkle with salt.

NUTRITIONAL INFORMATION, PER SERVING: about 160 cal, 13 g pro, 8 g total fat (1 g sat. fat), 8 g carb, 1 g fibre, 174 mg chol, 294 mg sodium, 402 mg potassium. % RDI: 5% calcium, 11% iron, 2% vit A, 25% vit C, 5% folate.

Spicy Fish and Chorizo Stew

HANDS-ON TIME	•	TOTAL TIME	•	MAKES
30 MINUTES		30 MINUTES		4 SERVINGS

What you need

2 tsp	olive oil
½ cup	diced dry-cured chorizo
1	onion, diced
¼ tsp	hot pepper flakes
2 tbsp	tomato paste
4	cloves garlic, thinly sliced
1	can (796 mL) no-salt-added diced tomatoes (see tip, below)
1	can (540 mL) no-salt-added white kidney beans, drained and rinsed
½ tsp	salt
340 g	skinless tilapia or other firm white fish fillets, cut in 1-inch (2.5 cm) chunks
½ cup	chopped fresh cilantro
2 tsp	red wine vinegar

How to make it

In large nonstick skillet, heat oil over medium heat; cook chorizo, stirring often, until lightly browned, about 3 minutes. Add onion and hot pepper flakes; cook, stirring occasionally, until onion is softened, about 5 minutes.

Stir in tomato paste and garlic; cook, stirring, until fragrant, about 1 minute. Add tomatoes; bring to boil. Reduce heat and simmer, stirring occasionally, until beginning to thicken, about 8 minutes.

Add beans and salt; cook, stirring occasionally, until heated through and stew is slightly thickened, about 5 minutes. Stir in fish; simmer until fish is opaque throughout and flakes easily when tested, about 2 minutes.

Remove from heat; gently stir in cilantro and vinegar.

TIP FROM THE TEST KITCHEN
Canned tomatoes and beans are typically high in sodium. Using no-salt-added varieties means you have more control over how much salt ends up in the finished dish.

NUTRITIONAL INFORMATION, PER SERVING: about 376 cal, 32 g pro, 13 g total fat (4 g sat. fat), 34 g carb, 9 g fibre, 61 mg chol, 645 mg sodium, 1,248 mg potassium. % RDI: 10% calcium, 49% iron, 22% vit A, 25% vit C, 12% folate.

Serve this spicy curry over fragrant steamed brown or white basmati rice.

Bengal-Style Fish Curry

HANDS-ON TIME	•	TOTAL TIME	•	MAKES
35 MINUTES		1¼ HOURS		4 OR 5 SERVINGS

What you need

SPICE PASTE:

1 tbsp	ground coriander
2 tsp	dry mustard
1½ tsp	chili powder
1 tsp	pepper
1 tsp	ground cumin
¾ tsp	salt

FISH CURRY:

675 g	skinless firm white fish fillets (such as tilapia or ocean perch)
1 tbsp	lime juice
1 tsp	turmeric
½ tsp	salt
¼ cup	vegetable oil
6	small dried red hot peppers
1 tsp	black or yellow mustard seeds
3	whole cloves
1	bay leaf
2	cloves garlic, pressed or pounded to paste
2 tsp	finely grated fresh ginger
1	onion, finely chopped
3 tbsp	plain yogurt
3	green finger chili peppers, halved lengthwise and seeded
	fresh cilantro sprigs

How to make it

SPICE PASTE: Stir together coriander, mustard, chili powder, pepper, cumin, salt and 2 tbsp water; set aside.

FISH CURRY: Cut fish into large chunks. Drizzle lime juice over fish; sprinkle with turmeric and salt. Cover and refrigerate for 30 minutes.

In skillet, heat oil over medium-high heat; cook fish, turning once, until golden brown. Using slotted spoon, transfer fish to plate; set aside.

Drain all but 2 tbsp fat from pan; reduce heat to medium. Cook dried hot peppers, stirring, until fragrant and slightly darkened, about 30 seconds. Add mustard seeds, cloves and bay leaf; cook, stirring, until seeds begin to pop, about 1 minute. Stir in garlic and ginger; cook, stirring, until fragrant, about 1 minute.

Add onion; cook, stirring, until golden, about 5 minutes. Stir in Spice Paste; cook, stirring, for 4 minutes. Stir in yogurt and ½ cup water. Add green chili peppers; cover and simmer for 5 minutes.

Return fish to skillet; cook, spooning sauce over top, until fish flakes easily when tested, 3 to 5 minutes. Discard bay leaf. Spoon onto serving dishes; garnish with cilantro.

TIP FROM THE TEST KITCHEN

Fresh spices have the best flavour. Buy small amounts and use them up within six months of purchase to ensure you're getting the most intense taste.

NUTRITIONAL INFORMATION, PER EACH OF 5 SERVINGS: about 220 cal, 29 g pro, 9 g total fat (1 g sat. fat), 7 g carb, 2 g fibre, 69 mg chol, 661 mg sodium, 570 mg potassium. % RDI: 6% calcium, 14% iron, 6% vit A, 8% vit C, 18% folate.

Coconut Curry Shrimp

HANDS-ON TIME
15 MINUTES

TOTAL TIME
20 MINUTES

MAKES
4 SERVINGS

What you need

⅔ cup	coconut milk (see tip, below)
1 tbsp	fish sauce
1½ tsp	mild curry powder
1 tsp	packed brown sugar
¼ tsp	each salt and pepper
450 g	large shrimp (31 to 40 count), peeled and deveined
1	sweet red pepper, diced
2	green onions, chopped
¼ cup	fresh cilantro leaves
4	lime wedges

How to make it

In large bowl, whisk together coconut milk, fish sauce, curry powder, brown sugar, salt and pepper. Add shrimp, red pepper, green onions and cilantro; toss to coat. Let stand for 5 minutes.

In wok or large heavy-bottomed saucepan, cook shrimp mixture over medium-high heat, stirring, until shrimp are pink and opaque throughout, about 6 minutes. Serve with lime wedges.

TIP FROM THE TEST KITCHEN
Use full-fat coconut milk for this recipe—and for all of our recipes—unless light coconut milk is specified.

NUTRITIONAL INFORMATION, PER SERVING: about 186 cal, 19 g pro, 10 g total fat (7 g sat. fat), 7 g carb, 1 g fibre, 129 mg chol, 626 mg sodium, 355 mg potassium. % RDI: 6% calcium, 28% iron, 16% vit A, 92% vit C, 11% folate.

Thai Curry Mussels With Bok Choy

HANDS-ON TIME	TOTAL TIME	MAKES
15 MINUTES	15 MINUTES	4 SERVINGS

What you need

900 g	mussels
1 tsp	vegetable oil
1 tbsp	Thai red curry paste
½ cup	coconut milk (see tip, opposite)
340 g	baby bok choy, halved lengthwise
¼ cup	chopped fresh cilantro

How to make it

Scrub mussels; remove any beards. Discard any mussels that do not close when tapped. Set aside.

In large saucepan, heat oil over medium-high heat; cook curry paste, stirring, until fragrant, about 1 minute. Stir in coconut milk.

Add mussels and bok choy; reduce heat, cover and simmer until mussels open, 5 to 8 minutes. Discard any mussels that do not open. Sprinkle with cilantro.

TIP FROM THE TEST KITCHEN
This recipe also makes an impressive appetizer; simply divide into six servings.

NUTRITIONAL INFORMATION, PER SERVING: about 153 cal, 10 g pro, 11 g total fat (6 g sat. fat), 6 g carb, 1 g fibre, 19 mg chol, 231 mg sodium, 638 mg potassium. % RDI: 10% calcium, 34% iron, 43% vit A, 48% vit C, 29% folate.

Sausage and Shrimp Gumbo With Okra

HANDS-ON TIME	TOTAL TIME	MAKES
25 MINUTES	30 MINUTES	4 SERVINGS

What you need

1 cup	short-grain white rice
2 tbsp	vegetable oil
3 tbsp	all-purpose flour
1	small red onion, chopped
1	rib celery, chopped
1	small sweet red pepper, chopped
2	cloves garlic, chopped
2 tsp	Cajun seasoning
1 tsp	smoked paprika
2 cups	sodium-reduced chicken broth
1	spicy dry-cured sausage, such as andouille or chorizo (115 g), chopped
1 cup	chopped fresh or frozen okra
200 g	medium shrimp (41 to 50 count), peeled and deveined
2	green onions, chopped

How to make it

In saucepan, cook rice according to package instructions.

Meanwhile, in Dutch oven or large heavy-bottomed saucepan, heat oil over medium-high heat; cook flour, stirring, until lightly browned, about 2 minutes. Add red onion, celery, red pepper and garlic; cook, stirring occasionally, until slightly softened, about 4 minutes.

Add Cajun seasoning and paprika; cook, stirring often, until fragrant, about 3 minutes. Stir in broth and ½ cup water; bring to boil. Reduce heat and simmer until slightly thickened, about 4 minutes.

Add sausage and okra; cook until okra is fork-tender, about 4 minutes. Stir in shrimp; cook until pink and opaque throughout, about 3 minutes.

Serve gumbo over rice; sprinkle with green onions.

TIP FROM THE TEST KITCHEN

To give this gumbo a real New Orleans–style twist, top it with a pinch of filé powder, which is made from ground dried sassafras leaves. But don't worry if you can't find it: This hearty stew is equally delicious without..

NUTRITIONAL INFORMATION, PER SERVING: about 472 cal, 21 g pro, 19 g total fat (5 g sat. fat), 54 g carb, 3 g fibre, 81 mg chol, 764 mg sodium, 421 mg potassium. % RDI: 7% calcium, 19% iron, 16% vit A, 63% vit C, 20% folate.

Cheesy Salmon Casserole

HANDS-ON TIME	•	TOTAL TIME	•	MAKES
25 MINUTES		55 MINUTES		6 SERVINGS

What you need

1¼ cups	elbow macaroni
⅓ cup	butter
½ cup	diced onion
1	clove garlic, minced
3 tbsp	all-purpose flour
1¾ cups	milk
½ tsp	Worcestershire sauce
1½ cups	shredded Cheddar cheese (about 120 g)
1 cup	sour cream
2	cans (each 213 g) red sockeye salmon, drained and flaked
1½ cups	fresh bread crumbs

How to make it

In large saucepan of boiling lightly salted water, cook pasta according to package instructions until al dente. Drain.

Meanwhile, in separate large saucepan, melt half of the butter over medium heat; cook onion and garlic, stirring, until onion is tender, about 4 minutes. Sprinkle in flour; cook, stirring, until light golden, about 3 minutes.

Gradually whisk in milk until smooth. Add Worcestershire sauce; cook, whisking constantly, until thick enough to coat back of spoon, about 4 minutes. Stir in Cheddar until melted. Stir in sour cream, salmon and pasta. Scrape into lightly greased 8-cup (2 L) casserole or baking dish.

Melt remaining butter; mix with bread crumbs and sprinkle over top of casserole. Bake in 350°F (180°C) oven until topping is golden and casserole is bubbly, 25 to 30 minutes. Let stand for 5 minutes before serving.

NUTRITIONAL INFORMATION, PER SERVING: about 548 cal, 30 g pro, 33 g total fat (18 g sat. fat), 32 g carb, 1 g fibre, 104 mg chol, 656 mg sodium, 443 mg potassium. % RDI: 45% calcium, 13% iron, 29% vit A, 3% vit C, 37% folate.

Smoked Salmon Pizza With Baby Kale Salad

HANDS-ON TIME	•	TOTAL TIME	•	MAKES
15 MINUTES		25 MINUTES		4 TO 6 SERVINGS

What you need	How to make it

SMOKED SALMON PIZZA:

350 g	prepared pizza dough
1 tbsp	olive oil
¼ tsp	pepper
½ cup	cream cheese, softened
4 tsp	lemon juice
1 tbsp	milk
150 g	sliced smoked salmon
¼ cup	thinly sliced red onion
2 tsp	capers, drained, rinsed and chopped
2 tsp	chopped fresh chives
½ tsp	pink peppercorns, crushed

BABY KALE SALAD:

1 tsp	olive oil
1 tsp	lemon juice
pinch	each salt and pepper
2½ cups	lightly packed baby kale

SMOKED SALMON PIZZA: On lightly floured surface, roll out or press dough into 11-inch (28 cm) circle. Transfer to greased pizza pan; prick all over with fork. Spread oil over dough; sprinkle with pepper. Bake on bottom rack in 500°F (260°C) oven until golden and crisp, about 12 minutes. Let cool.

Meanwhile, stir together cream cheese, 2 tsp of the lemon juice and the milk; spread over crust. Top with salmon, red onion, capers, chives, peppercorns and remaining lemon juice.

BABY KALE SALAD: In bowl, whisk together oil, lemon juice, salt and pepper; add kale and toss to coat. Serve on Smoked Salmon Pizza.

NUTRITIONAL INFORMATION, PER EACH OF 6 SERVINGS:
about 297 cal, 11 g pro, 15 g total fat (5 g sat. fat), 31 g carb, 2 g fibre, 28 mg chol, 579 mg sodium, 284 mg potassium. % RDI: 12% calcium, 18% iron, 33% vit A, 58% vit C, 29% folate.

Mini Fish and Vegetable Pies

HANDS-ON TIME	TOTAL TIME	MAKES
20 MINUTES	30 MINUTES	4 SERVINGS

What you need

FILLING:

2 tsp	unsalted butter
2 cups	sliced leeks (white and light green parts only)
½ cup	diced carrot
½ cup	diced celery
3	cloves garlic, minced
2 tbsp	all-purpose flour
¾ cup	sodium-reduced vegetable broth
¼ cup	milk
300 g	skinless cod or other firm white fish fillet, cut in 1-inch (2.5 cm) chunks
½ cup	frozen peas
2 tbsp	chopped fresh dill
4 tsp	lemon juice
2 tsp	Dijon mustard
¼ tsp	each salt and pepper

MASHED POTATO TOPPING:

2	russet potatoes (about 500 g)
¼ cup	milk
2 tsp	prepared horseradish
pinch	each salt and pepper

How to make it

FILLING: In Dutch oven, melt butter over medium heat; cook leeks, carrot, celery and garlic, stirring occasionally, until beginning to soften, about 5 minutes.

Add flour; cook, stirring, for 1 minute. Whisk in broth and ¼ cup water; cook, whisking, until slightly thickened, about 2 minutes. Whisk in milk. Remove from heat; stir in fish, peas, dill, lemon juice, mustard, salt and pepper.

MASHED POTATO TOPPING: Meanwhile, prick potatoes all over with fork. Microwave on high until fork-tender, about 7 minutes. Set aside until cool enough to handle. Peel potatoes; mash together potato flesh, milk, horseradish, salt and pepper.

TO FINISH: Divide Filling among four 8-oz (250 mL) ramekins. Spoon Mashed Potato Topping over top, spreading to edge. Bake on rimmed baking sheet in 425°F (220°C) oven until filling is bubbly, about 10 minutes.

TIP FROM THE TEST KITCHEN
For crispy golden tops, broil the pies for one to three minutes.

NUTRITIONAL INFORMATION, PER SERVING: about 257 cal, 19 g pro, 4 g total fat (2 g sat. fat), 38 g carb, 4 g fibre, 40 mg chol, 392 mg sodium, 1,000 mg potassium. % RDI: 11% calcium, 21% iron, 42% vit A, 47% vit C, 30% folate.

Baked Perch Rolls

HANDS-ON TIME	•	TOTAL TIME	•	MAKES
10 MINUTES		30 MINUTES		4 SERVINGS

What you need

4	anchovy fillets, minced
3 tbsp	minced fresh parsley
2 tbsp	minced shallots
1	clove garlic, finely grated or pressed
4 tsp	extra-virgin olive oil
2 tsp	capers, drained, rinsed and minced
2 tsp	lemon juice
¼ tsp	hot pepper flakes
¼ tsp	salt
4	skinless white perch fillets (each about 115 g)

How to make it

Stir together anchovies, parsley, shallots, garlic, 2 tsp of the oil, the capers, lemon juice, hot pepper flakes and a pinch of the salt.

Lay fish, flesh side down, on work surface; spread anchovy mixture evenly over top. Starting from narrower tail end, roll up fish around anchovy mixture; secure with toothpicks. Place in lightly greased baking dish; drizzle with remaining oil. Sprinkle with remaining salt.

Bake in 400°F (200°C) oven until fish flakes easily when tested, about 20 minutes.

TIP FROM THE TEST KITCHEN
You can substitute other thin fish fillets for the perch in this recipe. Try striped bass, tilapia or channel catfish.

NUTRITIONAL INFORMATION, PER SERVING: about 157 cal, 23 g pro, 6 g total fat (1 g sat. fat), 2 g carb, trace fibre, 103 mg chol, 404 mg sodium, 362 mg potassium. % RDI: 10% calcium, 11% iron, 4% vit A, 8% vit C, 5% folate.

Soy-Glazed Arctic Char

HANDS-ON TIME	•	TOTAL TIME	•	MAKES
5 MINUTES		15 MINUTES		4 TO 6 SERVINGS

What you need

2	skin-on arctic char fillets (each about 340 g)
2 tbsp	unseasoned rice vinegar
2 tbsp	sodium-reduced soy sauce
2 tsp	grated fresh ginger
2 tsp	liquid honey (see tip, below)
½ tsp	pepper

How to make it

Place fish, skin side down, on parchment paper–lined rimmed baking sheet. Whisk together vinegar, soy sauce, ginger, honey and pepper; brush over fish.

Bake in 425°F (220°C) oven until fish flakes easily when tested, 8 to 10 minutes.

TIP FROM THE TEST KITCHEN

When measuring sticky liquids, such as honey, mist the measuring spoon with cooking oil first. This keeps the honey from sticking to the spoon.

NUTRITIONAL INFORMATION, PER EACH OF 6 SERVINGS:
about 119 cal, 21 g pro, 3 g total fat (1 g sat. fat), 3 g carb, trace fibre, 61 mg chol, 263 mg sodium, 339 mg potassium. % RDI: 1% calcium, 5% iron, 2% vit A, 2% vit C.

Parmesan-Crusted Fish

HANDS-ON TIME	TOTAL TIME	MAKES
10 MINUTES	20 MINUTES	4 SERVINGS

What you need

2 tbsp	Balkan-style plain yogurt
½ tsp	Dijon mustard
4	green onions (green parts only), minced
1 cup	panko bread crumbs
¼ cup	grated Parmesan cheese
3 tbsp	butter, melted
4	skinless halibut or cod fillets (each about 140 g)
pinch	each salt and pepper

How to make it

In small bowl, stir together yogurt, mustard and green onions. In separate bowl, stir together bread crumbs, Parmesan and butter. Set aside.

Pat fish dry; sprinkle with salt and pepper. Arrange on parchment paper–lined rimmed baking sheet; spread yogurt mixture evenly over fish. Lightly press bread crumb mixture over top.

Bake on top rack in 425°F (220°C) oven until crust is golden and fish flakes easily when tested, 10 to 12 minutes.

TIP FROM THE TEST KITCHEN
Check the fish for any pin bones by running your fingers along the flesh. If there are any, simply remove the bones with tweezers or needle-nose pliers.

NUTRITIONAL INFORMATION, PER SERVING: about 297 cal, 33 g pro, 14 g total fat (7 g sat. fat), 7 g carb, 1 g fibre, 75 mg chol, 260 mg sodium, 709 mg potassium. % RDI: 15% calcium, 13% iron, 16% vit A, 3% vit C, 11% folate.

This crispy-topped white fish is a go-to weeknight main because it's nutritious, delicious and so easy to prepare.

Pistachio-Crusted Salmon With Garlic Rapini

HANDS-ON TIME	•	TOTAL TIME	•	MAKES
15 MINUTES		20 MINUTES		4 SERVINGS

What you need

4	skinless salmon fillets (each about 170 g)
pinch	each salt and pepper
2 tsp	Dijon mustard
¼ cup	shelled pistachios, toasted and coarsely ground
1	bunch rapini, trimmed
1 tbsp	olive oil
3	cloves garlic, minced

How to make it

Place fish on parchment paper–lined rimmed baking sheet; sprinkle with salt and pepper. Brush tops with mustard; sprinkle with pistachios, pressing firmly to adhere. Bake in 425°F (220°C) oven until fish flakes easily when tested, 12 to 15 minutes.

While fish is baking, in large saucepan of boiling salted water, cook rapini until tender-crisp, about 2 minutes. Drain; using tongs, transfer to bowl of ice water to chill. Drain well.

In large skillet, heat oil over medium-high heat; cook garlic, stirring, until fragrant, about 1 minute. Add rapini; cook, stirring, until heated through, about 3 minutes. Serve with fish.

TIP FROM THE TEST KITCHEN
To make this vitamin-rich dish a complete meal, serve with steamed mini potatoes tossed with olive oil and fresh herbs.

NUTRITIONAL INFORMATION, PER SERVING: about 382 cal, 35 g pro, 24 g total fat (4 g sat. fat), 6 g carb, 3 g fibre, 84 mg chol, 390 mg sodium, 922 mg potassium. % RDI: 13% calcium, 15% iron, 45% vit A, 68% vit C, 53% folate.

Sofrito Baked Shrimp

HANDS-ON TIME	•	TOTAL TIME	•	MAKES
15 MINUTES		1 HOUR		2 SERVINGS

What you need | How to make it

2	red-skinned potatoes, scrubbed and cut in scant ¼-inch (5 mm) thick slices
1 tsp	olive oil
¼ tsp	each salt and pepper
¾ cup	coarsely chopped sweet red pepper
½ cup	coarsely chopped Cubanelle pepper
½ cup	coarsely chopped red onion
¼ cup	packed fresh cilantro leaves
1 tbsp	lime juice
2	cloves garlic
¼ tsp	hot pepper flakes
1 cup	cherry tomatoes, quartered
225 g	jumbo shrimp (21 to 24 count), peeled and deveined

In bowl, toss together potatoes, oil, salt and pepper. Overlapping slices, layer potatoes in greased 8-inch (2 L) square baking dish. Bake in 400°F (200°C) oven until slices begin to brown at edges, about 30 minutes.

Meanwhile, in food processor, pulse together red pepper, Cubanelle pepper, red onion, cilantro, lime juice, garlic and hot pepper flakes until finely chopped, 6 to 8 times. Strain and transfer to bowl; discard solids. Stir in tomatoes.

Spread half of the tomato mixture over potatoes. Arrange shrimp in single layer over top; top with remaining tomato mixture. Bake until shrimp are pink and opaque throughout, about 15 minutes.

TIP FROM THE TEST KITCHEN
To make an even spicier sauce, add a quarter of a seeded jalapeño pepper to the food processor.

NUTRITIONAL INFORMATION, PER SERVING: about 423 cal, 46 g pro, 6 g total fat (1 g sat. fat), 45 g carb, 6 g fibre, 302 mg chol, 600 mg sodium, 1,542 mg potassium. % RDI: 14% calcium, 49% iron, 38% vit A, 312% vit C, 33% folate.

Glazed Salmon Bundles With Sesame Bok Choy

HANDS-ON TIME
20 MINUTES

•

TOTAL TIME
30 MINUTES

•

MAKES
4 SERVINGS

What you need

GLAZED SALMON BUNDLES:

4	round (8½-inch/21 cm) rice paper wrappers
¼ cup	shredded carrot
¼ cup	thinly sliced green onion
4	skinless salmon fillets (each about 140 g)
2 tsp	vegetable oil
4 tsp	hoisin sauce

SESAME BOK CHOY:

2 tsp	soy sauce
1 tsp	granulated sugar
1 tsp	unseasoned rice vinegar
1 tsp	sesame oil
1	clove garlic, thinly sliced
1 tbsp	thinly sliced fresh ginger
2 tsp	sesame seeds
450 g	baby bok choy, quartered

How to make it

GLAZED SALMON BUNDLES: Fill 10-inch (25 cm) pie plate with hot water; working with 1 at a time, soak rice paper wrappers until soft and pliable, about 30 seconds. Remove and arrange in single layer on clean towel; pat dry.

Sprinkle 1 tbsp each of the carrot and green onion in centre of each round; top with each with 1 fish fillet. One side at a time, tightly fold rice paper over fish.

In ovenproof skillet, heat oil over medium-high heat; cook bundles until browned and crisp, about 1 minute per side. Brush top and sides with hoisin sauce. Transfer to 400°F (200°C) oven; bake until slightly firm to the touch, about 7 minutes.

SESAME BOK CHOY: While fish is baking, whisk soy sauce, sugar and vinegar until sugar is dissolved.

In wok or large nonstick skillet, heat sesame oil over medium-high heat; cook garlic, ginger and sesame seeds, stirring, until golden, about 2 minutes. Add bok choy and soy sauce mixture; cover and cook until fork-tender, about 3 minutes. Serve with Glazed Salmon Bundles.

TIP FROM THE TEST KITCHEN
Drying the rice paper thoroughly after soaking helps you achieve a nice, crispy texture on the fish bundles.

NUTRITIONAL INFORMATION, PER SERVING: about 339 cal, 28 g pro, 18 g total fat (3 g sat. fat), 15 g carb, 2 g fibre, 70 mg chol, 364 mg sodium, 944 mg potassium. % RDI: 14% calcium, 15% iron, 65% vit A, 62% vit C, 43% folate.

THANK YOU!

Thank you to the excellent group that put this delicious fish and seafood collection together. It was, as always, a pleasure to work with each individual on this A-team.

My biggest thanks go to food director Annabelle Waugh, senior food specialist Irene Fong and food specialists Amanda Barnier, Jennifer Bartoli and Gilean Watts in the Canadian Living Test Kitchen. They are passionate about fish and seafood, and it shows in every Tested-Till-Perfect recipe in this essential volume.

Second, my gratitude goes to our art director, Colin Elliott, for his tasteful design of this book. He's so much fun to work with and always has fresh ideas that make our books sing.

Next, thank you to the talented photographers and stylists who created the beautiful photos for this book. Look right for the complete list of photographers and stylists who contributed to these pages.

Thanks to Gilean Watts for going the extra mile and helping with a final read of the pages. The same goes to our copy editor, Lisa Fielding, and our indexer, Beth Zabloski, who tightened and tuned every turn of phrase and made it easy for you to search for your favourite dishes in the handy index. Thanks also to Sharyn Joliat of Info Access, who created the detailed nutritional analysis for each of our recipes.

I'm grateful to our teams at Juniper Publishing and Simon & Schuster Canada for getting this book out and onto bookstore shelves across the country. Their behind-the-scenes work makes our jobs easier.

Finally, sincerest thanks to Canadian Living's group publisher, Sandra E. Martin, and content director, multiplatform editions, special issues and books, Jessica Ross, for their guidance and thoughtful input. It's wonderful knowing they're supporting us every step of the way.

TINA ANSON MINE
PROJECT EDITOR

RECIPES

ALL RECIPES Tested Till Perfect by the Canadian Living Test Kitchen.

PHOTOGRAPHY

RYAN BROOK p. 90.

JEFF COULSON front cover; back cover (left, second from top; left, bottom; far right); p. 6, 9, 16, 26, 41, 46, 51, 55, 56, 60, 78, 87, 99, 111, 115, 121, 129, 133, 141, 148 and 159.

YVONNE DUIVENVOORDEN p. 35, 36, 70, 105, 106, 116, 122 and 127.

JOE KIM p. 65, 95 and 134.

JEAN LONGPRÉ p. 15 and 77.

EDWARD POND p. 10, 20, 84 and 112.

JODI PUDGE back cover (centre); p. 30, 83 and 147.

TANGO PHOTOGRAPHIE p. 19, 29 and 74.

JAMES TSE back cover (left, third from top); p. 5, 25, 45, 89 and 100.

MAYA VISNYEI back cover (left, top); p. 142.

FOOD STYLING

STÉPHAN BOUCHER p. 77.

ASHLEY DENTON back cover (left, third from top); p. 5, 25, 45, 65, 84, 89 and 100.

CAROL DUDAR p. 147.

HEATHER ELOPH p. 41.

VÉRONIQUE GAGNON-LALANNE p. 19.

DAVID GRENIER front cover; back cover (left, bottom; centre); p. 30, 78, 99 and 159.

ADELE HAGAN p. 111.

MIRANDA KEYES p. 133.

LUCIE RICHARD p. 10, 20, 83, 106 and 122.

DENYSE ROUSSIN p. 15, 29 and 74.

HEATHER SHAW p. 115.

CLAIRE STUBBS back cover (left, top); p. 36, 56, 60, 70, 87, 105, 112, 116, 127 and 142.

MELANIE STUPARYK back cover (left, second from top); p. 26, 55, 90, 141 and 148.

NOAH WITENOFF p. 52.

LEEANNE WRIGHT p. 121.

NICOLE YOUNG back cover (far right); p. 6, 9, 16, 35, 46, 51, 95, 129 and 134.

PROP STYLING

LAURA BRANSON back cover (left, second from top); p. 55, 87, 90, 95, 106, 111, 115, 133, 134 and 147.

AURELIE BRYCE back cover (far right); p. 6, 9, 16, 26, 41, 121 and 129.

CATHERINE DOHERTY back cover (left, third from top; centre); p. 5, 10, 20, 25, 30, 35, 45, 46, 51, 65, 78, 83, 84, 89, 100 and 112.

VÉRONIQUE GAGNON-LALANNE p. 19.

MADELEINE JOHARI p. 36, 56, 60 and 141.

SABRINA LINN back cover (left, bottom); p. 99.

MONIQUE MACOT p. 15 and 77.

SASHA SEYMOUR p. 148 and 159.

CAROLINE SIMON p. 29 and 74.

OKSANA SLAVUTYCH p. 116.

CAROLYN SOUCH/JUDY INC. front cover.

PAIGE WEIR back cover (left, top); p. 142.

GENEVIEVE WISEMAN p. 70, 105, 122 and 127.

INDEX

Index

About Our Nutrition Information

To meet nutrient needs each day, moderately active women aged 25 to 49 need about 1,900 calories, 51 g protein, 261 g carbohydrate, 25 to 35 g fibre and not more than 63 g total fat (21 g saturated fat). Men and teenagers usually need more. Canadian sodium intake of approximately 3,500 mg daily should be reduced, whereas the intake of potassium from food sources should be increased to 4,700 mg per day. The percentage of recommended daily intake (% RDI) is based on the values used for Canadian food labels for calcium, iron, vitamins A and C, and folate.

Figures are rounded off. They are based on the first ingredient listed when there is a choice and do not include optional ingredients or those with no specified amounts.

ABBREVIATIONS
cal = calories
pro = protein
carb = carbohydrate
sat. fat = saturated fat
chol = cholesterol

Scallop, Sweet Pepper and Zucchini Salad
page 49

Canadıan Lıvıng

Complete your collection of Tested-Till-Perfect recipes!

Canadian Living: The Ultimate Cookbook

The Complete Chicken Book
The Complete Chocolate Book
The Complete Preserving Book

400-Calorie Dinners
Dinner in 30 Minutes or Less
Essential Salads
Fish & Seafood
Make It Chocolate!
Pasta & Noodles
Sweet & Simple

New Slow Cooker Favourites

The Affordable Feasts Collection
The Appetizer Collection
The Barbecue Collection
The International Collection
The One Dish Collection
The Slow Cooker Collection
The Vegetarian Collection

150 Essential Beef, Pork & Lamb Recipes
150 Essential Salads
150 Essential Whole Grain Recipes

Available wherever books are sold or online at
canadianliving.com/books